The TAO  of Conversation

How to talk about things
that really matter,
in ways that encourage new
ideas, deepen intimacy,
and build effective and creative
working relationships.

Michael Kahn, Ph.D.

NEW HARBINGER PUBLICATIONS, INC.

Publisher's Note

This publication is designed to provide accurate and authoritative information in regard to the subject matter covered. It is sold with the understanding that the publisher is not engaged in rendering pyschological, financial, legal, or other professional services. If expert assistance or counseling is needed, the services of a competent professional should be sought.

Copyright © 1995 Michael Kahn
New Harbinger Publications, Inc.
5674 Shattuck Avenue
Oakland, CA 94609

Cover design by SHELBY DESIGNS & ILLUSTRATES.
Text design by Tracy Marie Powell.

The publishers have generously given permission to use extended quotations from the following copyrighted works. From *The Complete Upmanship,* by Stephen Potter. Copyright © 1970 by Stephen Potter. Reprinted by permission of Henry Holt and Co., Inc., and by permission of Peters Frazer & Dunlop Group Ltd. From *Talking from 9 to 5,* by Deborah Tannen, Ph.D. Copyright © 1994 by Deborah Tannen, Ph.D. Reprinted by permission of William Morrow & Company, Inc. From *Talking Power,* by Robin Tolmach Lakoff. Copyright © 1990 by Robin Tolmach Lakoff. Reprinted by permission of BasicBooks, a division of HarperCollins Publishers, Inc.

Distributed in U.S.A. by Publishers Group West; in Canada by Raincoast Books; in Great Britain by Airlift Book Company, Ltd.; in South Africa by Real Books, Ltd.; in Australia by Boobook; in New Zealand by Tandem Press.

Library of Congress Catalog Card Number: 95-69487

ISBN 1-57224-029-6 hardcover
ISBN 1-57224-028-8 paperback

99   98   97

10   9   8   7   6   5   4   3

for Virginia

Contents

Preface   vii

Acknowledgments   ix

1   Conversation: Struggle, Small Talk . . . or   1
    Jam Session?

2   Free-for-Alls, Beauty Contests, and the   15
    Distinguished House Tour
    Idea Conversations

3   One-Up, One-Down, or Not Keeping Score?   41
    The Rationale for Cooperative Idea Conversations

4   Let Me Tell You What You're Doing Wrong   69
Relationship Conversations

5   We Had Spaghetti Three Times Last Week   91
Empathy

6   How Do We Get *Out* of Trouble?   105
Atonement

7   Will You Play Hamlet as Mad or Shamming?   117
Decision Conversations

8   Can I Really Do This at Work?   141
Conversations in the Business Environment

Bibliography   159

Preface

The ancient Chinese philosopher Chuang-tse told this story:

> The king, wandering through his kitchen, paused to watch a butcher cutting up a bullock.
>
> "I have been watching you for some time," he said to the butcher. "You never sharpen your knife like other butchers do. Why is that?"
>
> "Sire," said the butcher, "my father followed the Tao and taught me to follow the Tao. This knife belonged to him, and he passed it to me. He used it every day for many years and never sharpened it. You see, ordinary butchers hack their way through the animal. Thus their knife always needs sharpening. My father

taught me the Taoist way. I merely lay the knife by the natural openings and let it find its own way through. Thus it never needs sharpening."

The Tao (pronounced *dow*) is an ancient Chinese term that refers to the watercourse-like flow of nature. Flowing water (like the butcher's knife) never tries to batter its way through an obstacle, but finds its way around and through. Though the Tao flows gently, without contention, it is energetically engaged.

This book offers a way of conversing that is energetically engaged without struggle or contention. Its mantra might be "What a relief to discover that there's nothing to argue about."

I have been working on this book a long time. Over the years I have facilitated a good many human-relations training groups, and I have trained a large number of college seminar leaders. The people in my groups and seminars have taught me a great deal about the Tao of conversation. This book is an attempt to pass on what I have learned.

When conversation becomes a struggle, it can be very unpleasant. When conversation restricts itself to trivia, it can be pretty boring. It turns out those are not the only two options. It is possible to have a fruitful discussion of a difficult interpersonal problem, or to have a passionately engaged talk about politics, without argument or even disagreement.

That's what this book is about. I hope you find it interesting.

Acknowledgments

I have had good teachers. My fellow group-facilitators at the National Training Laboratories, and the countless participants in those groups, have taught me much of what I know about relationship conversations. I am particularly grateful to John and Joyce Weir and to Ted Kroeber who helped me conceptualize the principles of relationship conversations. Much of the rest of what I know about those conversations I have learned from the wonderful students who have been trained at the counseling center I direct at the California Institute of Integral Studies. They have participated in weekly human-relations training groups with me and met with me in a weekly group-leadership training seminar. They have taught me at least as much as they have learned from me.

My students at the University of California, Santa Cruz, worked with me for years figuring out the best way to conduct a college seminar. Much of what I know about idea conversations I learned with and from them.

Roger Fisher and Bill Ury have taught me about negotiation. My life-partner, Virginia Stutcki, read each chapter and made important suggestions. My friend, Jonathan Cobb gave me a great deal of indispensable guidance when I needed it most. Suzanne Derrer, Naomi Stoller, Jacqueline West, Andrea Panaritis, and John Boettiger have believed in the importance of the ideas in this book for many years; their support has been invaluable. My friend and colleague, Jack Clareman, has supported me through the writing of this book in more ways than I can name.

I am deeply appreciative of my publisher, Matt McKay for having had faith in this book from the beginning. My editor, Kirk Johnson, has worked devotedly to make the book readable.

1

Conversation: Struggle, Small Talk . . . or Jam Session?

A group of friends have just seen a movie together. John gets a brilliant idea about the structure of the movie. He sees just what the director was trying to do and just where he blew it and just how to fix it for him. The group sits at a table in the café, and he shares his discovery with the others.

Mary is startled.

She says, "Oh, I don't think that was what the movie was about at all. I think it was frankly meant to be a romantic fantasy, and I think it really succeeded in being that."

A couple of the others nod and agree with her view.

John says, "Well, let me tell you why I think that's not at all what the director had in mind. If it were meant to be just pleasant fantasy, it certainly wouldn't have included a character dying."

The others enter the discussion. They all support Mary.

What does John do now?

What he may discover is that he is rapidly talking himself into seeing this friendly conversation as a win-lose confrontation. At the moment, Mary is winning. She has dealt neatly with his position and gone on to offer one of her own that is receiving support and admiration from the audience. And so, resolving not to go down without a fight, John flings himself into the fray.

At this point, he is far past caring about which point of view is the more interesting, much less considering if they may even be compatible. This is a battle. And fighting a battle makes it all too easy for him to forget that he and Mary are good friends. He does his best to show her she is wrong. The others join Mary, and John digs in and fights grimly on, determined to hold off the entire army.

By the time the coffee is finished and the group straggles out, John is feeling terrible. Since he has made some of his points with a wounding aggressiveness, Mary is not feeling wonderful either.

In a situation like this it's hard to know who "won"—or even to know how to *tell* who won. From the outside, it looks like nobody has.

Here's another way to talk about ideas:

A father and teenage son have seen a play together. Driving home, the father says he liked the play. The boy says he did too. There is a silence.

The father says he particularly liked one scene and mentions it. Silence.

The boy says one of the characters reminded him of someone he knows. Briefly he tells his father about his friend. Silence.

They agree it was a good play. Silence. The subject changes to their plans for the weekend. Both feel dissatisfied and uneasy.

The second conversation is as *disengaged* as the first was *combative*. Both leave the participants unhappy.

Conversations like these don't have to be about *ideas*. Here is one about a *relationship:*

A woman meets a man she likes and with whom she hopes to explore a serious relationship. By the third date, she realizes that he needs to talk (a lot) about his previous lover. As the conversation proceeds, she finds herself increasingly angry.

She interrupts him to tell him that she finds this all very inappropriate. Why does he find it necessary to belabor her with the details of his painful breakup? He might notice she has the taste and courtesy not to do the same. She does not consider his previous relationship any of her business, and if he has to agonize about it, perhaps he could agonize with somebody else.

He replies that he thinks she's being just a bit jealous, and unnecessarily so, since the previous relationship is completely finished. He adds that he feels very close to her and that she is the person with whom he wants to share his stories—all his stories—and if she's not interested in supporting him, perhaps he has misjudged the relationship.

She replies with some heat that perhaps he has indeed misjudged her and perhaps she has misjudged him as well. At this point, a relationship that had looked extremely promising to both of them is in danger.

And here's another combative conversation in which a *decision* needs to be made:

A PTA group is trying to decide whether to advise the school board to drop competitive letter-grades for the very young children.

A teacher makes an impassioned speech strongly urging that there should be no grades for children below thirteen years old: grades are an unnecessary burden on them that badly distorts their view of learning.

A parent speaks equally passionately, arguing that removing grades means reducing standards and that the kids will be penalized when they are forced to compete later on.

The teacher suggests that the parent is being old-fashioned and authoritarian.

The parent calls the teacher lazy and sloppy and suggests that he's not willing to do the work of grading.

The teacher says a new system would be better because . . . and lists reasons. The parent says the present way is better and lists reasons. Other people join in, supporting one side or the other. The volume grows high and the tempo fast. Finally the meeting ends with no decision and a good deal of leftover acrimony.

Who Won?

Clearly, the participants emerge from all of these conversations feeling at least dissatisfied and in some cases actually feeling bad. It's also clear that the participants approached each other as if the only way for them to be engaged with each other was to be in conflict. It's not hard to understand why.

When my parents sent me off to college, the only piece of advice I remember—the advice that I suppose was meant to assure my social success—was "Never discuss politics or religion." Contained in that advice was the strong cultural belief that *combative* and *disengaged* are the only available conversational modes.

One can gossip or make small talk. One can tell stories or listen to them. One can take turns saying ideas that bear little or no relation to what the other person has said. But if you are to engage, really engage, that means combat.

A cruel paradox underlies this costly belief. Engagement is what makes interpersonal life worth living. How very painful, then, to believe that engagement must end by hurting and alienating one or both of us.

It's not surprising that our culture should view conversation that way. It is the way it views almost everything. The political scientist Andrew Hacker puts it this way:

> America has always been the most competitive of societies. It poises its citizens against one another, with the warning that they must make it on their own. Hence the stress on moving past others, driven by a fear of falling behind. No other nation so rates its residents as winners or losers. (*Two Nations*, p. 29)

We are a fight culture. We glory in competition, and we want to win. Our best-sellers carry titles like *Winning Through Intimidation*. We treat our elections as boxing matches, and our national leaders unhesitatingly set race against race and class against class as an election strategy. In public, our highways and city streets have become racetracks filled with angry competitors. At home, we entertain ourselves with television humor built around the putdown.

Sometimes the competition is civil, and sometimes it is brutal. Civil or brutal, the specter of violence is never far off. A corporate manager can get killed for an unpopular decision, as a San Francisco mayor was killed a few years ago for refusing to rehire an official who had resigned. Professors get killed for failing a student. People get shot in arguments over parking spaces. We have emerged from the decades of the Cold War to find ourselves in the midst of a dozen little hot ones, as though the species can't stand the thought of peace. Is it any wonder that we are raised to believe that the only way to avoid an argument is to restrict the conversation to trivia?

Is There a Point to This?

What is the purpose of conversation? Why do we engage in it at all?

Most of the time, we can identify two purposes: a substantive one and a purpose having to do with the relationship between the participants. The substance is what the conversation is about. I want to persuade someone or learn from someone or test an idea or work out a problem or make a decision. The relationship purpose is that I want to enjoy this contact with the other person or persons, and, with some exceptions, I would like this conversation to help us feel good about ourselves and about each other.

It's doubtful that the substantive purpose of a conversation is often served by combat; the next two chapters will explore that proposition at some length. And it's certain that all-out war does very little to build or preserve relationships, though it's easy to see how we get tempted into combat. We want so much to be heard and acknowledged that we'll even try the futile tactic of arguing our way to recognition.

Is it obvious why this is so? Let's suppose that there is a kind of conversation that is neither combative nor disengaged—a conversation that is more like making love.

One of the major differences between fighting and making love is this: if you and I are in a fight, I will feel good if you feel bad. The worse you feel, the better I feel. My feeling good *depends* on you feeling bad. On the other hand, if you and I are making love, I will feel good if you feel good. The better you feel, the better I'll feel. In fact, my feeling good *depends* on you feeling good.

A fighting conversation is by definition one in which we are each trying to establish that we are right and the other is wrong. Thus we are trying to defeat each other. Someone is likely to feel bad; in fact it would not be a surprise if both of us came out feeling at least a bit bad.

Now, undoubtedly we all have conversations with people we don't like or even actually want to hurt because we're mad and want revenge. We don't care about the future of the relationship and probably don't even expect it will have a future. If I were a saint, I would be able to work toward world peace by trying to create a loving relationship with such an antagonist. But I'm not a saint, and I just want to get him. This book is not about that conversation. Fortunately, for most of us, there are not many of those.

Most of our conversations are with people we don't want to wound and discard. And yet I get so caught up in the desire to be right, the desire to win, that at this moment being right is more important to me than how you feel. Winning, being right, seems now more important than the quality of our relationship. It also seems more important than the quality of the conversation and more important than my hope of learning something from it. What could have been an occasion for our learning from each other, for giving each other pleasure and validation, for deepening our relationship, has become a contest, a struggle. And the cause of social evolution will simply have to advance itself without our help.

Recall the earlier conversation in which the man jeopardized a new relationship by talking about his former lover. That same situation could have produced a very different conversation.

He tells her about his previous lover, and she replies that she can see how much pain he's still in from the breakup. And she can see how much he needs to talk to her about it. However, she adds, she is having a hard time with the conversation. She had hoped that she had at last found a man who wasn't looking for a mother. And now it seems that he wants her to take care of him.

He says that he can see what she means and that she's quite right: he feels wounded and would appreciate some caretaking. He adds that it's a little unnerving to be contemplating a long-term serious relationship with someone who doesn't want to do some caretaking.

She replies that one of the things that had attracted her to him was that he seemed such a caretaker himself. She's afraid that if she allows this relationship to start out with her in the caretaker role, she's never going to get out of it, and his demands will escalate until she gets fed up and kicks him out.

He says he can really understand that and can imagine that she's had some experiences that confirm that fear. He has no wish to make her his mother and have her do nonstop caretaking. Nevertheless, sometimes he does need to be taken care of, and he wonders if it's not possible for them to have a relationship in which each can get taken care of sometimes.

She agrees that the prospect of that kind of relationship doesn't seem so terrible . . .

. . . And war has been averted, clarity has been added to the relationship, and a loving connection has been made in the conversation.

Or recall the PTA argument. Suppose that the teacher had acknowledged the parent's concerns as legitimate, suggested that the question of giving young children grades is really a dilemma, and had wondered if the group could invent some way that would deal, at least a little, with the concerns on both sides. That acknowledgement and that invitation might have produced a very different conversation and a very different outcome.

The theme of this book is that just about any conversation is likely to turn into battle, *but* that just about any conversation can also be like making love. Here's one that showed all the signs of a potential war and turned out to be something quite different.

A man and a woman are seated next to each other at a dinner party. A turn in the conversation leads him to mention his anger at the anti-abortion activists who have been trying to shut down clinics. He's surprised when she replies that she feels quite sympathetic to them.

He expresses indignation and observes that the pro-lifers don't seem much concerned with life once it's born. She nods and says that's a good point. She goes on to say that they don't seem very compassionate toward the pregnant women either. Nonetheless, she adds, she does indeed believe that a fetus is a living creature and that killing it is horrifying to her. She says it gently and with unmistakable sincerity.

The man is struck by her sincerity and says so. He says that he's never actually talked to an anti-abortion person before. He is silent and thoughtful for a few moments and then says that he can indeed see it her way: if someone were killing six-month old babies for some desirable social end, he would be horrified. If she believes a fetus is just as alive as a six-month old baby, he can readily see how upsetting abortion would be to her.

She smiles gratefully at him and says that she in turn can see the terrible social cost of unwanted pregnancies. They agree that abortion is a complex problem with no perfect solution. Both feel stimulated and puzzled and very warm toward each other as they converse through the rest of the dinner.

It's all too easy to imagine how this might have gone. He could have been the one who pointed out the pro-lifers' lack of compassion for pregnant women, and she could have argued the analogy of the six-month old babies. What turned the conversation around was her generous acceptance of his point about pro-lifers not being very concerned about life once it's born. That took him off the defensive and left him in a position to really hear her emotional concerns. What marks this as a high-level conversation is that the people are not only listening to each other, but are actually helping each other build their case.

Of I and Thou

The Israeli philosopher Martin Buber provides a valuable point of view for this topic. Buber suggests that the civilized world is organized in such a way that we are all under great pressure to treat each other as objects, to create what he called "I-It" relationships. There is, he said, only one way to be saved, and that is to learn to create "I-Thou" relationships. An I-Thou relationship is one in which with all my heart I allow you your freedom, and with all my heart I accept and encounter you as you *are*, not as I would like you to be. Buber went on to assert that when two or more people encounter each other in this way, then, and only then, can life be deeply satisfying.

When you think about it, it seems intuitively true that Buber is right: we do in fact treat each other as objects much, perhaps most, of the time. And it does darken our world—in the streets, in our workplaces, and, most painfully, in our homes. And in asking us to change, he is asking a lot. He is asking us to give up the effort to control each other and *really* allow others their freedom. Not trying to control the way others think or feel, not judging their thoughts and feelings as wrong, trying only to learn their truth and accept it—that is very hard to contemplate. Yet Buber suggests that it is an absolutely necessary step if we are to evolve toward a more loving and peaceful way of being with each other.

In the realm of conversation, an I-Thou relationship would be one in which I neither tried to change your mind nor attempted to show you that you were wrong, but rather found my way to a genuine interest in your perspective—and to a willingness to help you grasp mine, should you be interested. From this point of view, a conversation would always have at least two goals: to increase our understanding of the topic and to improve our relationship. A person following Buber's path would want the other people to come out of each conversation feeling good about themselves.

The obstacle to this for most of us is that conversations seem to become contentious before we know it. In a subsequent chapter, we will examine the proposition that there is very little payoff in embattled conversations. People learn very little, they change their positions hardly at all, and they come out of the conversations feeling something between uncomfortable and terrible. Does it have to be this way? Is there another way to converse?

Just Jamming

Consider for a moment a group of musicians who have gotten together late at night, after their jobs are finished—who have gotten together to play for fun, that is, to have a jam session.

Sometimes the session starts with a standard tune, with everybody playing together, feeling their way, listening carefully to each other to see what is going on here tonight. And then, little by little, the musicians will begin to feel their way into their hearts, and improvisations will begin to circle around the tune. The players will improvise around the theme, talking to it, listening to it talk back, allowing their own unique creativity to shape it.

It is crucial that they are not playing by themselves; they are playing with other musicians, each of whom is also inventing interpretations of the theme. Now the players might compete for best interpretation, and being human they sometimes do. But that is not real jamming, and everybody knows that it's not.

Real jamming goes like this: you begin to feel your way to an interpretation of this piece. You hear your neighbor feeling her way to a different one. You listen hard as you play. She listens hard as she plays. Gradually or suddenly as you play you begin to hear the special magic of what she is doing and you begin to relate your interpretation to hers. Simultaneously she is hearing you and relating her interpretation to yours. And now the group's interpretation is not anyone's—it is everyone's. It would be difficult to say who started what or who thought up which part.

When musicians jam like this, some extraordinary works of art result. They have order and coherence and excitement. However wild the theme someone might introduce, his comrades will find some way of bringing it into the composition, of changing the composition so that it includes that theme.

Often one musician will get hot and take off on a solo ride. But it is never really a solo ride. It is influenced by what his comrades have been doing that started him on the ride, and it continues to be influenced by the way they are supporting him, backing him, riffing under him, playing quiet stuff around him. And if, afterwards, some listener compliments him on the solo, he will be pleased and accept the compliment, but he will al-

ways know that it was only an apparent solo, that it was produced by what his comrades had done before and what they
continued to do as he played, pulsing behind him, riffing under
and around him.

This is a way to think about conversation. It seems unlikely
that anyone would want to say that any one musician's interpretation of the tune was "right." What draws our attention is not
that there are right and wrong improvisations, but rather that
each one sparks and stimulates the others, and what emerges is
a composition that no one of the musicians could have done by
himself. Indeed, that is why they get together in the exhaustion
of the small hours when they might have been home. What else
prevents them from going home and playing their improvisations by themselves? What does prevent them is that they want
the spark and the stimulation of the other musicians in order to
join in the building of a composition farther out and more beautiful than any one of them could have done alone.

Critics are fond of saying that no work of art was ever
made by a committee. No jazz musician would ever have paid
the slightest attention to that notion.

The conversation about abortion showed us that a cooperative conversation can actually go beyond a mere tolerance for
the other person's position. The jam session is similarly instructive: a conversation can be an opportunity for us to spark new
understanding in each other, to stimulate and be stimulated,
and to join in building a position richer and more complete than
any we could have thought out on our own.

Of Him and Her

As we ponder how we're ever going to get out of the endless
contention and competition and find our way to cooperative
and loving conversation, it's instructive to recall that since the
sixties the women's movement has been pointing out that this
familiar battlefield is more of a masculine domain than a human
one. Women linguists, particularly Deborah Tannen and Robin

Lakoff, have shown how different men's and women's conversation styles actually are. Men's language has developed as an instrument of power—getting it, holding it, challenging it, defending it. It is the language of objectivity. Women's language has developed as a way of promoting collaboration and consensus. It is the language of interaction.

Lakoff says this about women's language:

> If jockeying for power and getting your directives
> obeyed are not your major priorities, you might
> develop a way of talking that stressed collaboration
> and consensus rather than hierarchical domination.
> You would have to treat others as individuals,
> respecting their rights and needs in communication,
> otherwise consensual decision is a travesty or an
> impossibility. Your arts and sciences would devise
> ways of winning others over to your thinking,
> cultivating the art of compromise and the science of
> management. You would have to become
> extraordinarily skilled in discovering what those you
> were working with wanted and needed, in order to
> keep the powerful placated, and your peers
> cooperative: a sixth sense that can be identified with
> "women's intuition," although it must be learned, if
> implicitly, and involves a wide array of complex
> talents. Women need to be in constant communication
> in order to keep the consensus stable and preserve
> feelings of trust. . . . Such communicative communities
> create bonds among their members and skill in
> interpersonal relations. The male analog is the power
> hierarchy for people, and mastery over things. As
> with every other difference between the sexes, the
> masculine prerogative has been exalted at the expense
> of the feminine. But the latter has always been the
> cohesive force holding communities together and
> staving off annihilation, even as men's ways bring us
> ever closer to the brink.

The ideal would be for both sexes to move their ways of communication closer to some middle ground. (*Talking Power,* p. 207)

It's fascinating to think that a way out of our embattled state is possible—if we can find a way of communicating that makes considerable use of the feminine modes of collaboration and consensus while maintaining the logic and clarity that has traditionally been thought of as masculine. Lakoff is not optimistic about this possibility, because such large parts of society have a stake in the status quo. But there is evidence that the picture is brighter than she fears. For half a century, both men and women have been discovering (in human-relations training groups and elsewhere) that there is such a meeting of the masculine and the feminine and that it is deeply satisfying. And for the last quarter century my colleagues and I have been discovering that that same meeting of masculine and feminine can make conversations about ideas equally satisfying to both men and women. Perhaps this meeting of the genders is the way out of the endless, wearying game of one-up and one-down.

We have looked at three kinds of conversation: conversations about ideas (the movie and the play), about relationships (the new love affair), and about decisions (the PTA meeting). We have seen how distressingly easy it is for any of those to become embattled, and we have begun to explore options to battle other than simply disengaging. In the chapters ahead we will see the costliness of believing it is important to be right and the even greater cost of our cultural addiction to the game of one-up. And we will explore the ways in which conversations can be like jam sessions where we let ourselves be stimulated and enlightened by the ideas of others.

2

Free-for-Alls, Beauty Contests, and the Distinguished House Tour

Idea Conversations

We have been considering the proposition that talking about ideas can be engaging and involving without being argumentative. But how? If you express an idea, how can I possibly respond without either nodding politely or challenging you in some way? How can I respond without simply "agreeing" with you, which would hardly move the conversation forward, or showing you some inadequacy in your idea, which is likely to lead to argument?

This chapter will propose that what I might do is join you in the building and elaboration of your idea. I might become your teammate, your colleague, your fellow musician jamming with you. We might wind up building a better idea than either of us could have worked out alone. Our conversation would be a living manifestation of the I-Thou relationship.

One of my academic responsibilities is leading discussions of ideas. For many years, when I polled my colleagues I found that many of us agreed that a college or graduate school seminar was apt to be one of two things: either a question-and-answer session or a series of arguments. Neither seemed very satisfying. And so some of us set about trying to learn how a seminar might work better. We assembled a group of interested students and began experimenting. What we learned completely changed the way I thought about idea conversations.

We discovered that there are four different kinds of seminars. We named the first three of them the *Free-for-All*, the *Beauty Contest*, and the *Distinguished House Tour*.

The Free-for-All. There is a prize out there in the middle of the floor. It may be the instructor's approval or it may be one's own self-esteem, but it's out there, and the goal is to win it. Anything goes—elbows, knees, gouging, anything. You win not just by looking smart, but by looking *smarter*. And that means that making *them* look dumb is just as important as making yourself look smart.

The Beauty Contest. There's a prize here too, but this time I try to win it by seeking your admiration. I parade my idea by you in its bathing suit and high heels. When it's off the runway, I go to the dressing room and get ready for my next appearance while you're parading your idea. Of course, I'm not paying any attention to your idea, and you're not paying any attention to mine.

The Distinguished House Tour. In most cities you can arrange to be taken on such a tour. You are driven to a stately home which is a good example of Edwardian architecture and furniture. The hosts have spruced it all up for your visit; they show you through and explain it all, and you ask questions. Then you get back into the bus and go look at another house, say one that is a good example of Georgian architecture.

In the Distinguished House Tour seminar, someone advances an idea. The rest of the seminar spends some time exploring her house. They ask questions, they explore for inconsistencies, and they try hard to understand the idea. When they have a good grasp of it, one of the other members offers another idea. It may be a whole different point of view on the same subject. The seminar members, including the first idea's hostess, then explore that house. The houses are not compared, nor does one person claim that his or hers is better. Each house is thought to be interesting in its own right and worth exploring.

My colleagues and I found the Distinguished House Tour to be a high form of discourse and one capable of producing an interesting seminar. It also has some significant problems.

In one of our early experimental seminars we were discussing Lao-tzu's *Book of the Tao*. One very young student said, "I think Lao-tzu's way is a good one—just going along minding your own business, not trying to tell other people how to live, not trying to organize the world, just looking after your own garden." We had been invited into her house, and we set about exploring it.

One of the members thought he found an architectural problem. In a friendly and helpful manner he said, "Yes, but what do you do when you discover that someone is mistreating a child? Do you mind your own business and let the child suffer?" Our hostess hadn't been in many seminars, and she had never before read this kind of book. The friendly question was all she needed to collapse and say, "Oh, yeah, I guess I didn't think it out very well."

She didn't speak for the rest of the seminar. No one felt good about it.

Later on, we invented the verb "socratease" to describe what happens when you ask friendly questions to show the holes in a person's idea. We realized that this young student had been badly socrateased.

Even in friendly territory, it's not just the young and shy who find defending or explaining a position lonely and stressful. It's lonely and stressful for almost anyone. It's lonely and stressful for me to feel the pressure of a roomful of people on me when I'm trying to explore a new idea in a seminar. At best it's like being a witness in a trial, and at worst it's like an inquisition. It's an adrenaline starter, not calculated to bring out my best thinking. Fortunately, we discovered a fourth kind of seminar. We called this one the Barn Raising.

The Barn Raising

When a family in frontier America needed a barn and had limited labor and other resources, the entire community gathered to help them build it. The family described the kind of barn they had in mind and picked the site; the community then pitched in and built it. Often neighbors would suggest changes and improvements as they built.

A Barn Raising seminar begins when someone brings the group an idea or asks a question. The original idea may be barely fledged and not at all thought out. It doesn't matter. The community gathers to build the barn, to put together that idea.

Suppose you offer an idea in support of Lao-tzu. Your idea may be one I believe and support, or one with which I disagree, or a totally new concept that I've never thought about before. In any case, your idea now becomes *my* project, and I set about helping you build it, helping *us* build it.

After you've offered the idea, you have no more responsibility for developing it, defending it, or explaining it than anybody else in the group. If I have a problem with the idea, the problem belongs to the whole seminar, not just to you. Whenever someone seems stuck and can't find any way to put a couple of bits of the architecture together, it becomes the task of the entire seminar to help him or her connect those two parts of the barn.

So you say that you think it would be desirable to wander through the world like Lao-tzu, leaving other people alone, and I want to help you build your idea, but I still can't bring myself to ignore the problem of the suffering child. I might say, "Okay, I'd like to develop that idea. But what if a child is suffering? That thought really troubles me. How do we deal with that, everybody? I need help." A third person might enter the conversation and say, "Well, as I listen to you two, it occurs to me we might handle it this way. Maybe Lao-tzu is saying that intervening will ultimately cause more suffering. Now if I have to set up a political system, and an army to defend it, in order to make sure that child doesn't suffer, there are surely going to be a lot more suffering children before very long. Painful as it is, maybe I'm better off with one mistreated child than with a whole Vietnam full of them. Does that help?" And there we are, building your barn.

An interesting thing about the Barn Raising seminar turned out to be that people didn't come out of the seminars with the same ideas they went in with. They learned, and they expanded their point of view. You may have heard the psychological principle that trying to persuade someone to accept an idea is a good way of stopping them from even considering it. What I *will* succeed in doing is entrenching that idea into my own head even more firmly. But if I make it my task to help build your idea, then my defenses are down, my creativity is mobilized, and the ground is fertile for learning.

Who Teaches? Who Learns?

Those are the four kinds of seminars we observed. No seminar is a pure case; they all go through periods of fitting into each of the categories. Sometimes they are unclassifiable. But the goal is to spend as little time as possible being stuck in a Free-for-All or a Beauty Contest, and as much time as possible raising a barn.

The conception that emerged from our experiments with college seminars was very similar to Plato's belief that we all know a good deal more than we know we know. Plato taught that there is deep wisdom buried in each of us, and it takes only friendly midwives to bring it to awareness. In our experimental seminars, people were repeatedly surprised by the quality of the ideas that they discovered in themselves. Everyone in the seminar was everyone else's teacher and also everyone else's student.

We also discovered that the participation of *every* member was important. In most groups, conversation is dominated by a few assertive and verbal people, and the only available points of view are theirs. One goal of our seminars was to maximize resources, and we found that the more widespread the participation, the richer the experience. Each consciousness is unique and irreplaceable, and when some people get shut out, the loss is significant.

The linguist Robin Lakoff teaches us what we must overcome to achieve the goal of widespread participation:

> In conversation, power is demonstrated by the holding of the floor. In general the one who has the floor the most, and/or is responsible for more successful topics than anyone else, has the most power—at least for the purposes of the conversation. . . . If topic choice is charted in mixed-sex conversation, men generally contribute the lion's share of "successful" topics. (A topic "succeeds" when others take it up; an unsuccessful topic is one that is broached and left to die. Women are responsible for an unusual number of these, largely because neither men nor other women are eager to take up women's topics, but everyone is more responsive to men's.) A speaker who has been made to feel powerless by the devices

mentioned will tend to become progressively more
silent as the conversation goes on, or at least will take
shorter and less assertive turns, thereby diminishing
her power still further. . . . To respond to someone's
topic signifies approval of both the topic and its
originator; to say nothing can convey the worst
kind of disapproval or lack of interest.
(*Talking Power*, p. 49)

Lakoff goes on to note that in ordinary conversation there
are two kinds of speakers: *involved* and *considerate*. People
whose conversational style tends to be involved are likely to be
aggressive and dominating, while considerate people tend to
hold back and appear less interested. What we have discovered
in our experimental seminars is that it is quite possible to defy
that correlation and be both involved *and* considerate.

I Came, I Saw, I Convinced

As the seminar experiments developed we realized that we
were learning not just about college classes, but about idea conversations wherever they might happen. Talking about ideas
can be pleasurable and stimulating. In fact, it can be among the
most pleasurable and stimulating activities we engage in. But
sadly it often isn't. It isn't because idea conversations are often
more like war than like love.

In many idea conversations, most of the time is spent trying to convince. *Convince* is an interesting word. It comes from
the Latin *vincere,* meaning *to conquer.* And so we talk about
ideas, and I try to convince you:

that I'm right

that I'm knowledgeable

that I'm clever

that I'm strong

that I am a person of conviction

and so on. And since convince means conquer, I not only try to convince you that I do possess those attributes, but that I possess them in greater quantities than you do.

The result is that most idea conversations carry a likelihood that the connection between the people may be damaged to some degree. At best, it is unlikely that the connection will be strengthened. Further, since we are trying to conquer each other, the desire for victory is stronger than the desire for learning, and not very much is likely to get learned. And since having my mind changed is apt to seem equivalent to having been conquered, I am very apt to do my best to come out of the conversation with the same ideas I went into it with. This does not seem like a prescription for pleasure and stimulation.

Here's an example of how we are taught to talk to each other about ideas. This is a fragment of a television discussion that aired on CNN's *Crossfire* on June 26, 1995.

Michael Kinsley: Let me try to explain to you what upsets me. It seems to me undeniable that what is being—the reason you are offended or I am offended or anyone else is offended by flag burning is because of the message it sends. It, therefore, is—it is speech in that sense, and if it—

Rep. Bob Barr: It's not speech.

Michael Kinsley: —if this—if people were only burning flags in private and no one could see it, no one would be bothered by it. It's the message it sends of contempt for the country, but that's exactly what makes our country great, is we protect people, even people who show contempt for it. Isn't that correct?

Rep. Bob Barr: No, that's not correct. I—if somebody disagrees with you so much that they want to go and punch you in the nose, does that make it okay simply because they're giving physical expression to the—to their freedom of expression? No, it doesn't. There's a big difference.

Rep. David Skaggs: There's absolutely no question that, in the current constitutional context that we're working in, flag burning, as awful and idiotic as it is, has been determined by the Supreme Court of the land to be political expression protected by the First Amendment. It falls within the speech clause of the First Amendment. That's why we're having this debate. Now it seems to me, in this era in which we are supposed to be conservative about basic American values, there is a high burden of proof on anybody that wants to amend the Constitution, a burden of proof that ought to be met by clearly demonstrating that there is some serious evil to be remedied or some major improvement in our constitutional order to be accomplished.

John Sununu: Why—but that's not going to explain why this has become partisan.

Rep. David Skaggs: It's not. It's not. This is a bipartisan—

John Sununu: —with the majority of Democrats on one side and the majority of Republicans on the other?

Michael Kinsley: Democrats have more sense. That's why.

John Sununu: Nonsense.

Rep. David Skaggs: But let me ask you, John, whether or not you think we should be really cavalier about amending the Constitution. What's the evil to be remedied here? What's the improvement in our Constitution to be achieved by this? Nobody can answer that question.

John Sununu: You don't feel—

Rep. David Skaggs: There have been three—

John Sununu: You don't feel; the symbolism of the flag—

Rep. David Skaggs: There have been three flag burnings in the last two years. What's the threat?

Rep. Bob Barr: That's a real interesting standard. That's a real interesting criteria. Before the Congress does something, we have to have a problem? We have to have somebody murdered before we make murder a crime?

Rep. David Skaggs: *(crosstalk)* Well, because it is the right of every minority that are being protected by the Bill of Rights.

It's impossible to imagine that any of these people learned anything from this exchange and very hard to imagine that any viewer was enlightened by it. It seems little more than kids facing off in a schoolyard. "Is so!" "Aint so!"

Wouldn't it be interesting to converse differently? Wouldn't it be interesting to go into an idea conversation not trying to convince, but rather trying to build the best idea structure that you and the other person or persons are capable of, just as if you had set out to improvise music or design a garden together? Wouldn't it be interesting to set yourself the goal of making the other person or persons feel smart, creative, and acknowledged?

Four Goals, Two Principles (and Some Attitudes)

The experimental seminars we did at Santa Cruz show the way to that kind of idea conversation. It works like this:

Both in and out of the academic world, most idea conversations are Free-for-Alls or Beauty Contests. Occasionally someone will act as an interested guest on a Distinguished House Tour. Very seldom does one person offer to help build the other person's barn. However, the seminar experiments suggest that all idea conversations, wherever they may happen and about whatever topic, *can* be Barn Raising conversations.

How is that accomplished?

Our work with the seminar suggests that it is helpful to enter an idea conversation with four goals:

1. To emerge from the conversation with different ideas from those held at the beginning.

2. To learn something new in the conversation.

3. To collaborate on building an idea better than either person could build alone.

4. To emerge from the conversation feeling good about oneself and about the other person.

It does not matter if the first three goals are not successfully met. If they are merely *pursued*, the fourth goal is sure to be met, and the conversation is very likely to be interesting.

To accompany the four goals, two principles emerged. (We will explore the rationale for these in the next chapter.)

1. *Right* and *wrong* are not useful concepts.

2. *Agree* and *disagree* are also not useful concepts.

And some attitudes:

1. Persuasion is not the goal.

2. The conversers are each other's teachers.

3. They are, of course, also each other's students.

4. People need reinforcement, recognition, validation. When an idea is interesting or helpful, it is important to acknowledge that it is.

5. Puzzlements, uncertainties, and questions are useful parts of idea conversations. Challenges are not.

6. It is helpful to pay attention to everything the other person says, even though that will sometimes mean deferring one's own idea or even losing it altogether.

How Is This to Be Done?

Here is what we learned in the experimental seminars.

First, it is helpful to start any idea conversation with a question.

Asking a question instantly establishes that I am not out to sell you anything, but rather to learn from you (or, more accurately, *with* you). The question can be one with far-reaching implications, or it can be as simple as "What do you think this movie was really about?"

Here are some examples:

Parents, after reading a bedtime story: "What is the message kids get from *Little Red Riding Hood?*"

A couple reading the newspaper together: "What effect do you think this controversy about gays in the military will have on the general level of tolerance in this country?"

Students in a religion class: "Do you think the idea of reincarnation does anything more than rationalize social injustice?"

Friends after a play: "Well, is Hamlet mad or isn't he?"

After watching a news program: "Do you think that world government is the only way to world peace?"

Once someone has offered a tentative way to think about the question, then that idea becomes the starting point for the structure we are going to build together. Once A has offered an idea, it becomes irrelevant whether or not B "agrees" with it. After all, agreement means little more than "At this moment, my limited vision happens to coincide with yours" and disagreement means "At the moment, my limited vision happens not to coincide with yours." All I have to do is make the reasonable assumption that there are more things in heaven and earth than are yet dealt with in my philosophy. Agreement or disagreement is not now the issue. A has staked out the site of the barn, and B has the opportunity to set about building it with her.

Let's look at an example. A and B are two friends taking a religion course together.

> B: Do you think the idea of reincarnation does anything more than rationalize social injustice?
>
> A: Oh, yes! I think it adds greatly to the sense of individual responsibility.

Now B has never entertained that thought before. In fact, B, who considers himself politically progressive, has taken a dim view of reincarnation for the reason implied in his question. It is naturally tempting for him to put forward his view. But this is a different game, and he resists the temptation.

> B: Hmm . . . Individual responsibility. The idea being that since I have to answer for my acts next time around I won't just do anything I can get away with? Like a belief in heaven and hell?
>
> A: I hadn't thought of it that way, but sure, that too. I was thinking that if I don't leave this world after death, but am going to be here for a long time, I take more responsibility for what happens to it.
>
> B: I can see that. That's interesting. I am more apt to litter a highway I'm just passing along, than to litter my own street.

B's statement, "That's interesting," is important. It says that B is really listening to A. Acknowledging the other person's idea or contribution also says that this is a conversation designed to make us both feel good about ourselves; it is not a battle.

There are now several possibilities. The conversation might continue along these lines, further developing this main theme. Or B might remind A of the original question.

> B: Well, what do you think? Do you think the downside of the reincarnation belief is that it rationalizes inequality and injustice?

B has cooperatively built A's idea and now invites A to reciprocate. This is a valuable opportunity for A. It gives her a chance to explore an idea new to her, secure in the assurance that she is not setting herself up to be put down.

She accepts the invitation.

A: I certainly see what you mean. I guess the idea is that I don't have to worry about people born in poverty since they brought it on themselves in a previous life.

B: Sure. And I don't have to feel any guilt or responsibility about my own fortunate circumstances since I earned those in a former life.

A: I do see that. But maybe that's a terrible misuse of a philosophy that ought to imply just the opposite.

B: How do you mean?

A: Well, even if I'm a fortunate person, I should still want to keep improving my karma. If I don't want to wind up a cockroach, I'd better work very hard for those less fortunate.

This seems very unlikely to B. He is tempted to challenge it. He has a thought he cares about, and yet he doesn't want to turn this into an argument. He decides to enlist A as a teammate.

B: Well, look, here's the problem I'm having with this. The people I know who believe in reincarnation, and admittedly it's a tiny sample, would never think that the way to a better incarnation is through social service. They think of more meditation and more spiritual study and more withdrawal. They believe that people in monasteries have the best prospects of all. I suppose such people do less harm than most, but they don't do much *good* for any-one but themselves. Do you think that's true? And if it's true how can we work that into your notion about increased responsibility?

B has found a good solution. He presents himself as A's teammate with a problem that the two of them, working together, need to deal with.

> A: Well, I think that is true for a lot of people who hold this belief. And your point about them doing less harm than most seems relevant. It's tricky, isn't it? On the one hand, you can't fault the serious meditators too much. They aren't doing harm, and they are putting positive energy into the world. On the other hand, you're right that it is pretty self-interested. My best guess is that these meditators wouldn't be doing a lot of social service if they weren't meditating. And I do know that there are a lot of people holding these views who believe in what they call *karma-yoga*—which means "the path of action and good works." So do you think we could say that the net result is positive?

A has picked up B's teammate model and in her last sentence asks for continued collaboration. Also, by saying "On the other hand you're right . . ." she acknowledges B's contribution, reinforcing the solidarity of the team and making a sincere move toward enhancing B's self-esteem.

> B: Maybe. I'm not sure it's true that the quietist types wouldn't be of much use out in the world. I think that if we are to establish that Eastern thought produces a social plus at the bottom line, we have to deal with the possibility that a lot of young people get hijacked by Eastern thought when they might otherwise have gone into a more socially useful line of activity, or at least developed a more socially useful philosophy.

The team is now firmly established. B could have merely presented his last point as a challenging argument, but instead he presents it as a problem for the team. Conversing this way encourages people to listen to each other and acknowledge each other's contributions. This is a contrast with the Free-for-All or the Beauty Contest, in which people are apt to get the uncomfortable impression that no one is really listening at all.

> A: You know, this may be an empirical question. I really don't know whether you're right that the majority of reincarnation believers are part of the problem rather than the solution. I suppose it's true in much of India. At least it's true that in India reincarnation is a rationalization for the caste system. But whether any of that is true in this country I simply don't know. I would like to think that being a long-term resident of the earth makes you more responsible, but I don't know if it does for many people.

> B: I don't either. I guess it is an empirical question. Anyway, I like your notion that since I'm going to be here for many lifetimes I had better take good care of it all. That's nice; I hadn't seen that before.

It's hard to imagine that an argument would have produced any more interesting thought—and even harder to imagine that an argument would have produced as good feeling between these people.

You can see the principles that emerge from this kind of conversation:

1. Whatever another person says is to be thought of as material for the ultimate composition. So each contribution has to be listened to carefully and thought about.

2. When an idea is offered, all participants have the opportunity to join in to improve, enlarge, or elaborate it.

3. The person who originally offered the idea has no more responsibility for it than anyone else. Questions about it or objections to it must be dealt with by everyone. The originator is as free to participate in this as anyone.

4. Sometimes it is appropriate for the team, working together, to build a case.

Suppose parents have read their child to sleep with *Rumpelstiltskin*, and, when alone, find themselves discussing the story.

A thinks this is a puzzling story. She thinks the Queen is a welsher and that Rumpelstiltskin gets horribly mistreated. B sees it differently. He thinks that Rumpelstiltskin has crossed the line of human compassion to even think of taking the Queen's child away. A suggests that they try building both cases, and B agrees.

It's helpful to imagine a couple of lawyers building a case. It's quite irrelevant to those lawyers what their "opinion" of the case might be. They have been hired to make the most convincing case possible for their client. So A and B, like a couple of smart lawyers, set out to make Rumpelstiltskin's case. The task of finding evidence in his defense is apt to become so interesting that B quickly forgets that this was not his original position.

A: The Queen made a fair bargain. She was in desperate need of help and was willing to pay for it. Rumpelstiltskin was a lonely old man who wanted a child. He bargained for it the only way he could.

B: I can see that. He didn't kidnap the child or hurt the mother. It's true. He had no way to get a child except to use his skill of spinning gold.

A: Right. And there's no indication that he had any malevolent intentions toward the child. Maybe he was just lonely and liked kids.

B: You know, another thing that supports this is that he had every right just to take the child without further negotiations. But he allowed the Queen the opportunity of guessing his name. He didn't have to do that.

A: Right. I don't think he's a bad guy at all. I think it's terrible that we're supposed to be glad he gets killed.

B: That was fun. Want to build the other case?

A: Sure. You start.

B: Well, put yourself in the young woman's place. He has her totally over a barrel. She's going to be killed if she doesn't produce the gold.

A: But he didn't put her in that spot. Her father did that to her.

B: Wait a minute! We built that case. Come on. Help with this one.

A: Sorry. Okay. Well, it is true. She didn't get herself in that spot. She was altogether at the mercy of the King and her father. So she had to agree to anything Rumpelstiltskin demanded. And I guess it really was pretty cruel of him to take advantage of her helplessness.

B: You bet. He demanded one of the most terrible things that can be asked of a woman—to give up her child. And he knew she couldn't refuse.

In a conversation such as this one, it's often interesting to see if it's possible to discover that the two points of view are not necessarily opposed but can be integrated into a synthesis. It can't always be done, but it's fun to try.

A: Well, look, maybe we're both right. You could say that he does begin by fair bargaining. He starts by accepting jewelry—which he obviously can't need very much if he can spin gold—and it's unfair to punish him for that. But he crosses the line of decency by upping the ante when he demands the child.

B: That's good. It makes him a kind of tragic hero, doesn't it?

A: Sure. Because he was so lonely he crossed some line of human decency and suffered for it. You know, no one actually hurts him. He destroys himself in a fit of rage. He really is a tragic hero.

> *B:*   Right. It's the same kind of injustice that happens in
>   *Oedipus*, where the hero was even more innocent.

By this time it doesn't much matter who started with what opinion. There has been no temptation to conquer, only the pleasure of improvising a composition together and the excitement of exploring the ideas it suggests.

Am I Being Flexible? Or Just Plain Wishy-Washy?

For some people, the whole notion of a collaborative idea conversation raises this question. If I have been taught that the strong and admirable thing to do is "stick to my guns," it may be difficult for me to fit conversations like these into my self-image. But "wishy-washy" is a pejorative description of an attitude which could just as easily be described as *flexible*. And what is considered sticking-to-my-guns by one person could seem like unnecessary rigidity to another.

When a decision has to be made, a point comes in the decision-making process when it is costly to vacillate. A person who vacillates at such a time might well be described as wishy-washy. But since, by definition, no decision need be made in an idea conversation, flexibility is a valuable asset. This is an important distinction.

In our experimental seminars we learned that people often confuse decision conversations and idea conversations. And the participants in an idea conversation often act as though a decision must be made. Does belief in reincarnation foster or hinder social responsibility? Is the moral of the fairy story this or that? Similarly, we often act as though the firmness and constancy so valuable in decision making are requirements in an idea discussion. The language is full of expressions supporting this belief: "He knows his own mind," "He has the courage of his convictions," and, indeed, "He's not wishy-washy." Perhaps we would be better off if we reserved the courage of our convictions for decision and action, and developed flexibility and fluidity in our idea conversations.

None of this is to imply that I shouldn't tell you my position at the beginning of a conversation, if I do indeed have one. If the conversation is about politics or religion or about a book I know well or about some aspect of my own field, it is likely that I will begin the conversation with an opinion about it. In such a case, it's important for me to lay my cards on the table, at the same time making it clear that I am in this conversation to explore your ideas as well as my own, to build ideas new to us both if possible, and that I am most certainly not planning to *argue* my position.

Political conversations are likely to produce arguments because they stir strong feelings. We've seen what a political discussion looks like on television. Let's look at another way of talking about politics.

> A: What did you think of the president's speech?
>
> B: I'm a groupie. I thought it was terrific. How about you?
>
> A: When I first heard it I was snowed by the salesmanship of it. But after I'd thought about it for a while I didn't like it at all.
>
> B: Why not? What didn't you like about it?
>
> A: I think that under all the glitz it was just the old Democratic stuff. He broke his promise to cut taxes for the middle class, and he's *really* reneged on the deficit reduction.

B is indeed a groupie. He has an immediate visceral response to what A has just said. His inner voice is full of energetic, not to say annoyed, response. But he chooses not to put himself and A, whom he likes a lot, into one more familiar and fruitless political argument. He ponders a moment and decides that both of A's charges have merit.

B: I certainly agree that he didn't offer the middle class a
        tax cut. And you're right that it was a major
        campaign promise. Guilty as charged on that one.

A: That's a big admission for a groupie. What about the
        deficit-reduction promises?

B: Well, he's in a serious bind. He's got to increase
        employment and still cut the deficit.

A: I think what's really going on is that he's chicken to
        cut social programs. And he's not going to get
        anywhere with the deficit if he doesn't.

How does B avoid a fight now without simply changing
the subject? How does he interest A in raising the conversation
to a higher level?

B: Sure, I suppose it could be some political caution.
        Look, let's switch to a wider angle lens. I think you
        and I represent two different points of view. You see
        the country's economic problems as having been
        caused by carelessly throwing money at the problems
        of the poor people. And you don't think that's money
        we can afford.

A: That's true. And I also think that what they're spend-
        ing is money that I worked my butt off to earn. I re-
        sent being made to support people who won't work.
        Our friend Carol has the same education we do and is
        a hell of a lot smarter than either of us, and she has
        never worked a day in her life. She keeps having
        babies by different men, secure in the knowledge that
        the taxpayers will support her. And we do— indefi-
        nitely. I resent the hell out of it.

B: I get it. I know that's your point of view. And I must
        say that I resent Carol too. Sometimes it looks like she
        has babies just in order to keep the support coming.
        I think your viewpoint has a lot of merit. Some of the
        welfare fraud is infuriating. And it *is* maddening to
        work hard and be made to support people who are
        laughing at us and who think we're idiots. But I also

have another take on the whole thing. May I try to
interest you in it?

A: Sure.

B: There are thousands and thousands of people who
are not in Carol's position and not in yours and mine
either. They can't make it without government help.
They need training and jobs and social support and
food stamps and money. You started with nothing
and made a good deal of money, and you don't see
why they can't do the same. But you were born white
and middle class in a decent neighborhood with a
mother who expected you would get an education
and do well. Can you imagine what it would be like
to start in the ghetto?

A: I know. That's true. I grant you all that. What I object
to is the Democrats playing to the poor people for
their votes without making any of the distinctions
we're talking about. It's cynical, and it robs me.

B: I think there's something to that. I don't pretend the
Democrats are selfless saints who just want to do
good.

A: And I agree that it isn't right to let kids grow up in
real poverty without anyone trying to help.

The argument has been avoided. The truth of the matter is
that there are probably few idea conflicts in which one side is
right and the other wrong. The world seems not to have been
put together that way. There is almost certainly a good deal to
be said on the other side of any position I hold, and asking
myself to explore that other side would be good exercise for my
mind. That is true whether I am discussing a movie or being
tempted to defend a cherished political opinion.

During the Cold War I was involved in the disarmament
movement. I believed that the presence of weapons makes it
likely someone will use them. I was also persuaded that arma-
ments represent an intolerable economic and political burden

for the world. Those who believed otherwise said that weakness invites attack and that this is a dangerous world. They suggested that I wouldn't walk through Central Park at night unarmed, would I? For years I fought these arguments and countered them with elaborations of my own position. I told my opponents that they were wrong and dangerously misguided. What's more, they used to make me very mad.

Well, today I think they were right all along. I think I was right too, but those on the other side weren't misguided (and probably some of them were not even in the pay of the munitions makers). If there's a course we can take that maximizes our "national defense" and minimizes the dangers, reasonable people can honorably disagree as to what that course is. But there simply is no either-or, yes-or-no solution. So it's not helpful to think of disarmament as a problem. It is, in fact, a dilemma.

Whose Dilemma Is This Anyway?

This is the classical embodiment of a *dilemma:* the ancient Greek hero Odysseus must sail a narrow passage between Scylla and Charybdis. Scylla is a monster who will pluck some seamen off the ship, and Charybdis is a whirlpool which will take the ship down. No course will avoid both of them. Sometimes it is possible to choose the lesser of the evils; better a few seamen than everyone on board. But there's no course that will bring everybody safely through. Some decisions must be made, and a price will have to be paid for either of the only choices that are available.

The notion being developed here is that for all practical purposes there are *no* problems that are not dilemmas. There simply is no solution to any of them, just as there is no solution to Odysseus's problem of Scylla and Charybdis. How shall we assure adequate warning of incoming planes or missiles? Well, how about radar sites spread throughout the country? That sounds like a fine solution. But then it turns out that large numbers of powerful radar sites fill the surrounding environment with a good deal of very dangerous radiation. Well, what shall it be: missiles without warning or a sharp increase in cancer and heart disease?

I used to work at a college whose governing body consisted of students, faculty, and staff. The rules once were that whoever showed up constituted the governing group for that session. Each time it met, a few new people were present. We got very little work done because at each meeting all the previous ground had to be covered anew to fill in the newcomers. It was a chaotic situation. The solution was to close the committee to new members once the school year had begun. But then it was no longer a committee anybody could influence. It was a closed group, an elite, and our democracy quotient went down markedly. Well, what shall it be, less democracy or chaos?

My credit card tempts me to solve my problems by borrowing. Well, what shall it be: poverty now or interest tomorrow? What shall it be: loneliness with freedom, or company with constrictions? And so on and on.

In the meeting at which my college attempted to resolve the issue about its governing body, everybody talked as though there were a problem to be solved; each speaker, myself included, offered the perfect solution. What nobody said was that there was no sense trying to solve the problem at all; it was a dilemma and all the impassioned arguments on both sides were perfectly correct. Had we ever acknowledged that, a lot of the heat would have cooled, and we could have proceeded from the agreement that there was cost in any choice; we were just playing Scylla and Charybdis.

This sense of a dilemma can be even more dramatic in an idea conversation where no decision need be made. Imagine you have just read Shakespeare's *Henry IV, Part I,* and settle down to discuss it with a friend. Many discussions about this play turn around the question of honor. You may recall that the play has several honor-preoccupied warriors and one powerful character, Sir John Falstaff, who sees honor as empty and dangerous. Now suppose your friend takes the position that this play teaches the foolishness of pursuing honor. You're not anxious to embark on an argument, nor are you anxious to deny yourself the chance to learn something that could come from exploring your friend's view. The trouble is you don't see it her way. You believe that honor is what distinguishes civilized life, that there can be no beauty or trust without it, and that Shakespeare is showing the contemptibility of Falstaff's cowardice.

Now at this point it would helpful for some muse of conversation to descend, alight on your shoulder, and whisper in your ear that the question of honor is a dilemma. Some rigid conception of American honor was at least partly involved in the madness in Vietnam, and, in this play, honor gets some beautiful young men killed over trifles. On the other hand, a startling *lack* of honor has cost us dearly in our government and generally makes life in this country very difficult. The dangers of street crime and of buying a used car are only two of a discouragingly large number of examples. And in this play, one reason these lamented young men were so beautiful is that their short lives were so charged with honor. So between the two of you, you and your friend are building a fine picture of the dilemma that surrounds honor. Were you to cooperate with each other, you might even find that the play supports both views: risking one's life for honor might be simultaneously beautiful and foolish, that is, tragic.

Conversations in which dilemmas emerge are particularly interesting ones. It is stimulating and engaging for everyone to join in building first one side of the dilemma and then the other. Such a conversation reliably produces more interesting ideas than an argument does. And the ultimate opportunity in such a conversation is to turn the dilemma into *dialectic* by making one side thesis and the other side antithesis and seeing if a synthesis can be found. That is high-level conversation, indeed.

Resisting the temptation to argue is not easy. We are raised to believe in right and wrong and to believe that to the victor shall go the spoils. It is hard to remember that no one wins most arguments. And it is still harder to remember that even if one were to "win," that victory would be a small pleasure indeed next to the joys of playing with ideas and of helping one's friends feel good about themselves.

3

One-Up, One-Down, or Not Keeping Score?

The Rationale for Cooperative Idea Conversations

As we consider these issues, the distinction between an idea conversation and a decision conversation becomes crucial. It is a distinction to which we will return. For now let's simply note that an idea conversation is one in which no decision need be made. Yet in idea conversations we tend to forget that we need not carry the burden of decision.

If you and I get into an argument about whether or not Hamlet is mad, we act as though a decision had to be made. Is he or isn't he? To tell the truth, the world will little note nor long remember whose argument carries the day (assuming either does), but you and I are likely to remember how we treated each other and how we felt afterwards. Whereas had we remembered that we enjoyed the luxury of not having to make a decision, we might have taught each other a good deal about the play and had a good time in the process.

I want to suggest that there is very little payoff in embattled conversations. People learn very little, they change their positions hardly at all, and they come out of such conversations feeling something between uncomfortable and terrible. So why on earth do we persist in having them?

It's easy to see why people play chess or tennis. The rules are clear, the competition circumscribed, and winning and losing are clearly defined. Most often the players are there to challenge each other for mutual growth and pleasure. After you have trounced me at chess or tennis, I may feel that my skill leaves something to be desired, but *I* am not disgraced. My sense of myself remains intact, and my identity is unharmed. Apparently that is not the case in a conversation.

Why do we struggle so with each other in situations where we know from experience that nobody is going to profit or feel very good when it's over? What makes it so hard to conduct a conversation such that we emerge feeling good about ourselves and each other?

The Conversational One-Up Game

The English humorist, Stephen Potter, has an answer to that question. Potter has written several books with titles such as *Gamesmanship, Lifemanship,* and *One-Upmanship,* all manuals on how to be one-up and how to avoid being one-down. Here are a couple of examples from *The Complete Upmanship.*

Potter on the practice of medicine, a discipline he calls "Doctorship":

> Doctor may *under certain circumstances* ask Patient his symptoms. But he will let it be seen that he is not listening to what Patient is saying, and may place his hand on Patient's wrist, or, better, stomach, as if to suggest that he as Doctor can tell more through the sensitive tip of one finger than from listening to the layman's self-deceiving, ill-observed, and hysterically redundant *impressions* of what is wrong with him.
>
> Many good MD-men make a point of shepherd- ing their patients into the consulting-room where, by his way of averting his head as Patient is undressing, Doctor can suggest criticism of his choice of under- clothes, socks, etc. The Doctor is well; Patient is ill: and (if only because he is longing for a cigarette) in more ways than in mere physical health. (p. 178)

And on religion:

> Countering and cross-countering in the more serious conversations reach extraordinary depths among advanced Lifemen. The ensuing notes are condensed from my Brochure.
>
> *How to Make People Feel Awkward About Religion.*
>
> The man who lets it be known that he is religious is in a strong Life position. There is one basic rule. It is: Go one better. Fenn went too far. This is his method—in his own words:
>
> To take the most ordinary instance—the simple Sunday churchgoer. "Are you coming to church with us?" my host says. It is a little country church and my host, Moulton, who has some claims to be a local squire, wants me to come, I know, because he is going

to read the lesson. He reads it very well. He enjoys reading it. I heard him practicing it to himself immediately after breakfast.

"Yes, why don't you come to church for once, you old sinner?" Mrs. Moulton will say.

Do *not* mumble in reply to this: "No, I'm afraid . . . I'm not awfully good at that sort of thing . . . my letters . . . catch post."

On the contrary, deepen and intensify your voice, lay your hand on her shoulder, and say, "Elsa," (calling her by her Christian name perhaps for the first time):

"Elsa, when the painted glass is scattered from the windows, and the roof is opened to the sky, and the ordinary simple flowers grow in the crevices of pew and transept—then and not till then will your church, as I believe, be fit for our worship."

Not only does this reply completely silence opponent, but it will be possible to go out and win ten shillings on the golf course, come back very slightly buzzed from Sunday pre-lunch drinks, and suggest, by your direct and untroubled look, before which their glance may actually shift, that by comparison with yourself your host and hostess, however innocently, have only been playing at religion.

That is Religion Basic. A harder character to tackle is the man of big personality with a grave, good-looking, rather biscuit-coloured face who digs himself in, so to speak, by being tremendously understanding and humorous, and by letting it be known that he belongs to a Group, and you needn't talk to him about it unless you feel like it.

The basic counter is, of course, to ask him about it almost before you have got into the room. Get him to explain, and after a few sentences say,

"Yes. Indeed I agree. I expect we all of us do. The

only trouble is, it doesn't go far enough. In other
words it's not a religion. It's an ethic. And a religion is
what we want. Now many of us . . . ," and then get
going.

This works with the layman, but many an expert
in Religionship is, in fact, an expert Lifeman of the
first water.

If so he will seem to appreciate and indeed
admire your answer and reply, "Good. Good. Good.
I'm not sure I don't rather agree." Leaving you
completely stuck. (pp. 92–93)

In spite of the tone, Potter is not kidding—any more than
Jonathan Swift was kidding. Like Swift, he is a trenchant social
satirist. Potter may be the writer to help us understand why it is
we pick hopeless fights with someone who otherwise would be
our valuable teacher.

Potter tells us that the great principle of lifemanship is "If
you're not one-up, you're one-down." That means you can't be
neutral, and you can't not play the game—you had better be
one-up or else. You know you're one-down when you're feeling
inferior, clumsy, awkward, foolish, embarrassed, at-a-loss, having to ask for help, feeling like you've lost an exchange. You're
one-up when you're feeling the opposites: superior, graceful, in
command, that you have won. Potter's great principle of lifemanship translates into "When you're not feeling superior, victorious, etc., you are by definition foolish, vanquished, etc." The
key variable in all this is *comparison*. One-up and one-down both
only mean something relative to someone else. In order to be
one-up, it is absolutely necessary to put someone one-down. In
fact, the only way I can possibly know whether I'm one-up or
not is to compare myself to the other person. If he's one-down,
I'm one-up. If he's one-up, I'm in trouble. (Andrew Hacker sees
the roots of racism in this phenomenon.) It's not hard to see why
putdowns, disparagement, and criticism are so common.

Potter's principle can be annotated like this: If I'm not feeling superior, graceful, in command, I am necessarily inferior,

clumsy, and foolish. That is a state to be avoided, and so I struggle to feel superior and victorious. The only way I can tell whether or not I've succeeded is to feel superior *to* someone, victorious *over* someone. So it is necessary to set out to make the other feel inferior, clumsy, and foolish.

We opened this book by overhearing an argument about a movie. John had a problem because his idea was in danger of losing. But the problem can exist even without that danger. Suppose John hadn't said *anything* about the movie, and Mary had simply launched her interesting analysis. When John recognizes how good her point of view is and watches their friends admire her, he still has the same problem: Mary is looking too good; she is one-up.

According to Potter's great principle, Mary's success has to mean that John is now one-down, and the only way he can rectify this situation is to challenge Mary. But, Potter reminds us, in order to be truly one-up, the putdown must be accomplished subtly. The game has to be played with apparent friendliness, and we can't ever look as though we're playing.

Potter presents a compelling case that the need to be one-up is such a ubiquitous and invariant motivational pressure that the one-up game is *the* great secret of human interaction. No matter what game is apparently being played, the real underlying game is one-upmanship. This point of view suggests that even though I tell you that I'm really playing friendly Conversation About a Movie (and really want a fruitful conversation for us all), what I'm in fact playing is One-Up. I simply cannot consider the possibility of having a pleasant and fruitful discussion with you until my superiority is established beyond question. And since my superiority is hardly ever *that* firmly established (there is always another fast gun just around the corner), I can never fully relax and allow myself to enjoy the conversation and our relationship.

Thus the interpersonal world is a jungle in which the law is: put down or be put down. But the residents of this jungle must all pretend that there is no such law and that they really live in a civilized world of friendship and cooperation.

Think about the last several arguments you were in and ask yourself why you were in them. The argument might have been about an idea, or it might have been about an issue in an important relationship, or it might have been about a decision that had to be made. In that argument, what was the likelihood that you were going to convince anybody of anything? Would it have made any difference if you had? If the likelihood was not high, was your motivation to be found in Potter's law?

When we look at the world in this way, it seems we are locked in an endless game. Unlike tennis, chess, and other in-the-open games, this one is a terrible burden. And how it does interfere with conversation!

Do I Want to Learn, or Do I Want to Win?

This question can be posed at any given moment in a discussion of ideas. Do I want to have a good discussion about this movie, or do I want to win? We can't do both; it's necessary to choose. The same question can be asked in a conversation about our relationship, about the feelings we have for each other or a conflict between us. Do I want us to be closer, or do I want to win? Do I want us to work it out, or do I want to win? Or in a decision conversation: do I want us to arrive at the best decision, or do I want to win?

Mostly the answer to the question seems to be that I would be happy to converse *after* I have won. I might be happy not to worry about winning *if* not winning didn't mean that I have to lose. But the jungle being what it is, I had better win first, and only *then* think about getting on with the conversation.

The irony of all this is that I *say* I want to converse, yet I *act* like I want to win. But this sort of winning is hardly satisfying; what would bring me satisfaction and make us both feel better about ourselves is exactly what I say I want—a friendly conversation—but dare not risk (for fear of losing).

The conversational one-up game wouldn't be quite so bad if it were played in the open like chess. That's the way one-up is played in a formal debate. But played in disguise, the game becomes a great burden.

Doesn't it seem that reasonable creatures like ourselves should be able to find a way to handle this differently? Since the jungle ethic is so enervating and so profitless, you'd think we'd give it up. When I'm confronted by my wife or a friend or a colleague developing a new idea, how much richer my life would be if instead of automatically criticizing the idea (or derogating it as commonplace) I enthusiastically joined her and helped her go on developing it. When we have a problem or a disagreement, how much richer our relationship would be if, instead of trying to prove myself right I tried hard to see the issue from her point of view before asking if she'd like to see it from mine. We would be contributing to the evolution of the species.

Survival of the Loudest

How can we explain our addiction to the one-up struggle? What started it and what keeps it going? Certainly there is a large evolutionary component to it: we are descended from members of the species that *won* the struggle for survival. The next generation is always sired by the strongest and most aggressive bull, and the best hunter survives to pass his strength and aggressiveness on to his children. The fact that we're here at all means that our genes are filled with competitiveness. Every species shows it, as does every culture in our species.

It's something like being addicted to sugar. We're descended from ancestors for whom a sweet tooth was a valuable way of distinguishing nourishing foods from poisonous ones. Now that the environment has changed and the candy rack in the supermarket has replaced the fruit tree and the berry bush, it would be far better if we were not drawn so inexorably to the Hershey bars. But how could our genes know that? Maybe in thousands of years the children of chocolate eaters will all have died out, but for now we simply have to struggle against a genetic tendency that used to serve a good purpose but that has become maladaptive.

I don't complain about the competitive genes; were it not for them we wouldn't even be here. Yet it does seem that the time has come to deal differently with them, to learn to let them express themselves by playing chess or tennis and watching football games, and to keep them from interfering so excessively with our relationships and our conversations and our general peace of mind.

In addition to that evolutionary component, there is also a large component related to our childhood socialization. All of us started our lives as very small creatures being raised by very large creatures. What the big people said, went. They told us what to do, and we did it. We told them what to do, and usually they didn't do it. If they did, it was apparent that they were doing it because they wanted to, not because they had to. In short, those big folk were permanently one-up and we were permanently one-down. In this world composed of big people and little people, of one-uppers and one-downers—it's likely that we saw you had to be one or the other and we vowed that once we were given the chance we were going to get out of our one-down position as fast as possible and not go back to it ever again without one hell of a struggle. That sort of very early learning is powerful, and it's reasonable to assume that that experience made a lasting impression on us.

My Opinion, Right or Wrong

Our addiction to one-upmanship makes it very tempting for us to argue about ideas. Another attitude which contributes to this is our conviction that something is either absolutely right or absolutely wrong. There is a right way to think, a right way to see the world, a right ethic, a right morality, a right politics. It's extremely difficult to *know* what's right because different authorities tell us different things. But we know that there *is* a right way and that it is important that we find it.

Parents suspect there is a right way to deal with the dilemma of freedom and discipline. Few are sure what that right way is, but most are convinced that there is one. Most of us are sure that there is a right way to govern a country or conduct an advertising campaign or to understand the nature of God. Sometimes we think we have found this right way, and that's a great relief. More often we are made uncomfortable by the suspicion that we haven't yet found it and that things won't be safe until we do. But that there is a right and wrong way few of us doubt.

Just as it's important to win, it is also important to be right. If my view, my idea, my ethic, my morality, my politics are different from yours, one of us is right and the other is wrong. If you are right, I am wrong, and that feels bad. And since there is nowhere I can go to look up the correct answer, I must do my absolute best to convince you and any other listeners that I am right and you are wrong. Most importantly, I must convince myself.

This right-or-wrong dichotomy leads to the illusion that the way to test an idea is to try it out in battle with a rival idea and see if it can win. College seminars are not the only instances of this sort of scrap; fights over ideas are likely to happen whenever an idea gets presented.

Is it true that a battle is the best way to test an idea? It may be true that if you bang baseball bats against each other the best one will emerge unshattered. But is it true of flowers for instance? If you bang one brand of rose in full bloom against another, one or both is likely to get knocked to pieces. It is not clear that this was an appropriate test of the beauty of the two flowers. A battle may not be an appropriate test of the beauty of two ideas either. It may test the power and aggressiveness of the arguers. It may test their shrewdness as they play to the prejudices or weaknesses of the judges or audience. But it seems doubtful that it's a reasonable test of the relative merits of the ideas.

This doubt leads to another question, this one very complex. Should ideas be pitted against each other at all? If we can agree that battle may not be a good place to compare ideas, let's take the next step and ask whether ideas should be compared at all.

I think Hamlet is a play about a son's guilt over unconscious erotic feelings toward his mother, i.e., the Oedipus Complex. I understand the play best in that light. You think Hamlet is a play about the paralysis and indecision of the intellectual and understand it best that way. I have a lot of evidence for my view. You have a lot for yours. We could fight it out, playing for the approval of an audience. We could duel it out in a discussion group, playing for the approval of the teacher. We could argue it out by ourselves, trying to put each other down and raise questions the opponent cannot answer. "Ah ha, Hamlet is a paralyzed intellectual, is he? Well, how do you explain the murder of Polonius? How do you explain that, huh? I have you, don't I? Well, *my* theory can explain that." And so on.

Now suppose we agree that a battleground is not the best place for literary criticism. We wouldn't bang roses against each other, would we? So we work out another way: we each write a paper complete with arguments and evidence and ask a competent judge to read them both and pick the right one.

You see what this assumes. This assumes there *is* a right one. The battlefield question simply asks whether fighting is a good way to get at the best idea. Now we need to ask whether there is a best idea. Most of us were taught in school that indeed there is. That seems to be a pivotal assumption, one well worth examining.

Is It Useful? Is It Beautiful?

Perhaps the best way to ask the question is to ask whether it is *useful* to behave as though there is a right idea. The implications of behaving as though ideas are right or wrong are clear: they lead to ideas being treated like gladiators or like cakes being judged at a state fair. But what happens if we try on the assumption that ideas are not right or wrong and explore the implications of that assumption? I think I can make it a bit easier for you to try that assumption on by sharing a couple of discoveries that have made adopting it considerably easier for me.

I went to a graduate school in which I was trained to believe in scientific truth. That is, when the results were analyzed by the proper statistical methods, a carefully done experiment would reveal the truth. It was many years later that I stumbled onto a philosophy of science called *conventionalism* and discovered that some modern scientists, those white-coated pursuers of truth, had entirely turned away from the notion that right and wrong were attainable concepts. It was a shock, I confess.

The notion of these workers was that the history of science reveals the laboratory to be a fine place to find out how *workable* some technique is, but a poor place to learn whether a theory is true or false. For instance, we might use the lab to test whether some drug cures diseases in mice, and find out that the drug does cure them, but that result can't prove or disprove my theory of how the mice got sick and what makes them well. That theory is a harmless little poem which will never be proved and which can be contradicted by a dozen experiments anytime anyone sets her mind to it. If I do a critical experiment proving for all time that my theory is true, I will find in the next edition of the journal a critical experiment proving an opposing theory equally true. There is, these scientists maintain, simply no way of ever establishing whether a theory is true or not.

That proposition leads the conventionalists to the question of how we decide whether or not to adopt a theory. Since we'll never know if any theory is true or false, we need some way of deciding which of all the possible theories we shall adopt. The conventionalists offer us two criteria for the adoption of a theory:

(1) Does it work? Is it technologically useful? Does it permit me to cure the disease or build the bridge? I may have a fantasy about *why* it works, and that fantasy might amuse the Great Scientist in the sky, but in practice all I need to know is if it *does* work.

(2) Is it beautiful? Does it turn me on? Is it a way I want to look at the world, and at my fellow creatures? Since all theories are equally true and equally false, I might as well choose one that makes my world beautiful. One theory of people says they're essentially evil and need to be transformed. Another says they're essentially good and need only to be left alone. It seems unlikely that either of these theories will ever be proved true or false. Therefore, say the conventionalists, let's by all means pick the one we like, the one which delights and stimulates us and makes the world most rich and most beautiful.

Now, if even some *scientists* are abandoning the notion that there is a right and a wrong . . .

You can see the relevance of this proposition. If ever I could be freed from having to:

prove I'm right

prove you're wrong

decide which of our competing views is right

then new possibilities open up. We can experience the phenomenon of discussion in a new way. If your view is different from mine, once I'm freed from the "rightness" problem I can listen to it with considerable interest to see if it contains some beauty or delight for me. It may turn out to be so beautiful and delightful or happen to work so well that I find myself abandoning my old view. Or I may well find that both views (however contradictory) have something helpful or something pleasing to contribute, and I may want to entertain them both. How much broader it would leave my mind to be continually aware that there is no problem, that I need not choose between your thought and mine, and that both thoughts can coexist with profit.

Spinach and green onions do a good deal better when planted with each other than either does separately. It's often true of ideas, too.

But if ideas are not right or wrong, how shall we talk about them? In preparation for answering that question I would like to offer a set of propositions.

1. If ideas are not right or wrong, there is nothing to fight about. In our culture, ideas have become a prime arena for the one-up game. As early as the third grade, we learned how important it was to have the right idea and to be the first one to have it recognized. Most of us were taught long before college that everyone in a discussion was a rival and that our score depended as much on showing our rivals to be wrong as on showing ourselves to be right. It's not enough to seem smart; it's necessary to seem *smarter,* and if possible *smartest.* By the time most of us got out of college, we didn't know there was any other way to talk about ideas. Arguing and trying to win seemed the only way to have a truly engaged idea conversation.

2. Fear and anger in any amount inhibit thinking. Practically all of us were educated in a tradition which didn't seem to understand that simple fact. Most educators seem to operate on the premise that the best way to stimulate a person's ideas is to attack the person. A mind under attack dare not be lazy, or so the argument goes; it must wake up and fight for survival. The attack may take the form of an aggressive challenge or a question that subtly suggests there is something wrong with the idea. However attractive this view of mental stimulation might be to educators, it is not supported by the findings of experimental and physiological psychology.

Let's approach it this way: in professional football, coaches like to see their linemen good and mad before a game and even madder during it. They are not above whipping up some of this anger by whatever means come to hand. The lineman has a relatively simple task; at a given signal he has to try to beat the hell out of the guy across from him. If he's mad, he is likely to win that fight. His juices are flowing and he's formidable.

The quarterback is a different story. Coaches are not given to getting their quarterbacks mad. In fact, an angry quarterback is a cause for some concern to his coach. This is so because the quarterback has quite a different task from the lineman. Each time his team is about to put the ball in play, he must decide which of about two hundred plays he's going to use. He must make this decision by calculating more than a dozen variables, and he has about ninety seconds to do so. At the end of this ninety seconds, his work is nowhere near done. He must participate centrally in the play, which often ends with about six hundred hostile pounds crashing down on top of him. Then he must get up, shake his head, and set about making the next complex decision. Plainly, he needs to be calm and alert, and it is commonly agreed among athletes and their coaches that fear or anger are not helpful to such a player at such a time.

All of us can identify with the quarterback's situation. When do you do your best thinking? Do you do it when you are scared or mad, or when you are free of either of those emotions? Do you think most creatively when the environment is friendly, or when you are being hassled?

It is axiomatic in aviation circles that what kills pilots is adrenaline. A pilot gets into an emergency, the fear shuts down his or her ability to think creatively or even reasonably, and the emergency escalates into a disaster. This happens even though he or she has responded smoothly to simulations of that emergency dozens of times in practice. It's simply easier without the adrenaline.

The physiological psychologists have given us a useful explanation of this phenomenon. A portion of the midbrain is known as the *reticular activating system.* (It is called that because the intricate network of nerves resembles an old-fashioned network handbag called a reticule.) One of the functions of this part of the brain is to receive messages from the upper brain concerning potentially emotion-arousing perceptions. These messages are then sent on to the blood vessels, the heart, the lungs, and the muscles, which respond with the classic fight-or-flight arousal pattern. (Very good, if you're a lineman!) The message comes back to the reticular formation that the body is mobilized; it sends word up to the forebrain that an emotion has indeed been aroused. Part of the this upward message takes the form of a massive electrical discharge across the forebrain, which is the part of the brain with which we do our complex thinking. This massive discharge functionally (if temporarily) damages the forebrain and reduces its power to carry on complex thought. When the emotion subsides, the brain returns to its full potential.

What this means is that a conversation in which I am continually in danger of being attacked, or a conversation in which I have been attacked and am fighting back, is one in which I am functioning on some small fraction of my thinking potential. The same adrenaline that kills pilots gives us a good reason to think of ourselves as stupid.

Although a good deal of psychological research suggests that fear and anger are detrimental to thinking and creativity, there is one large area of confusion among psychologists who concern themselves with this subject. The confusion goes like this: while it is widely agreed that *too much* arousal is disorganizing, it is also agreed that *too little* arousal is likewise bad for performance. People who are asleep or very near it are not good at tasks requiring alertness, thinking, and talking about ideas. We don't want our quarterback angry, but we don't want him calm to the point of boredom and disinterest either. These factors led psychologists to conclude that there is an optimal degree of arousal for any given task; it mustn't be too little or too much.

All this seems clear enough; the difficulty comes from an old and persistent assumption in psychology that all arousal is the same. Indeed, many different kinds of arousal—fear, anger, excitement—do have very similar physiological concomitants. As a result, many psychologists have continued to believe that it doesn't much matter what *kind* of arousal is involved as long as it is the right *amount*.

When educators applied the psychologists' findings, they came up with the notion that a little anxiety in the classroom probably was a good thing. It kept the kids on their toes, kept the juices flowing. Nobody ever argued the kids should be paralyzed with large amounts of fear—just a nice moderate dose. The same has been reasoned about anger. You probably don't want to get students very angry—for one thing, it isn't safe—but attacking them a little ought to stimulate them to fight back and stir themselves to optimal levels of arousal. Similarly, if you could stir up a little healthy competition between them, it ought to have a salutary effect.

The trouble with all this is that there is simply no research to support it—and a good deal to contradict it. The original research that generated these notions was done with animals, and it was performed by experimenters whose theories held that *drive* (another name for arousal) was a unitary concept: fear, anger, hunger, all contribute to the amount of drive present. A rat that hasn't eaten for 24 hours will run a maze for food very much like a rat will run a maze to get away from a cat; the drive to do so, the animal psychologists thought, is something that can be increased by deprivation or fear or anger, and it will look just the same no matter which emotion has caused it.

Psychologists who work with humans borrowed this concept, partly because it is so tidy. This probably wasn't a very helpful decision. The evidence is all against it: no one has ever shown that small amounts of fear or anger improve complex mental activity in humans. And there is all kinds of evidence that creativity and thinking suffer as those emotions are introduced.

Moderate levels of arousal are clearly needed for optimal thinking, for optimal learning, and for successful talking about ideas. But, and it's a big one, that arousal can't come from fear or anger. Fear and anger, in any amounts, interfere with the brain functions necessary for thinking or conversing.

Evolution favors survival, and the history of our species indicates that fear and anger have a more urgent survival value than creative thought has. When I am in danger, my attention goes to that danger, rather than to some idea. If the danger is not very great, only some of my attention goes there; as the danger increases so does the amount of preempted attention, and that is attention I don't have available for thinking.

When my attention is so directed, I use it to scan the environment for cues relative to that danger. I cannot scan for cues relative to the idea we are discussing unless things around me are obviously safe enough to let me take my radar set off border patrol and put it to work on the idea.

So where shall we find the arousal necessary for thinking and conversing? Some of it certainly comes from *involvement*—involvement with other people, involvement with ideas. Some of it comes from the excitement of seeing our horizons expand, at seeing a little farther into the vastness. Some of it must come from the fun of building ideas together with our friends—the excitement of creation.

There is another source as well: the breaking down of existing mental structures is itself arousing. If I come into a conversation convinced that the book I have read is a simple treatise on the history of tea drinking, and you surprise me by sharing your understanding of its wide social and spiritual implications, my present mental structure breaks down. That breakdown is arousing; it is accompanied by the same physiological indices we noted earlier.

What happens to that arousal depends on the context of the conversation we're having. If it's followed by the perception that I am stymied and at a loss to incorporate this new point of view, that arousal will be unpleasant and disrupting. So if you tell me that I've stupidly missed the point of the book and then walk out of the room, or if you interrupt me or argue with me each time I try to build a new mental structure which will include the new insights, the arousal will likely turn into frustration and anger. But if this is truly a friendly or loving conversation in which I feel safe and that my contributions are welcome, then the arousal is exciting. Now there is something I can do with it. I can enjoy your new perception and set about shaping it with you. In time, it becomes a new structure in my head.

It is important to note that a truly friendly or loving conversation is *not* one in which I blandly accept everything you say in order to avoid upsetting you. That is an easy confusion to get caught in. Such a conversation would put us all to sleep. And it wouldn't even be very loving, since my unthinking agreement indicates that I really don't care enough about your idea to help you shape it. As we will see, a loving conversation is one in which we cooperate in continually changing our mental structures.

3.   When we argue, we are not in an I-Thou relationship. The most important thing in our lives is how we treat each other. However much different religions and ethical systems disagree about most things, they all place a high priority on our relations with each other. It would certainly change the quality of our lives if we could treat everybody we meet with loving respect—the people we pass on the street, the people we wait on in stores or restaurants, and particularly the people who wait on us. And it would certainly improve our lives if we could extend that modest courtesy to the people close to us, the people we converse with. Sometimes it is very hard to do. Sometimes it requires considerable greatness of spirit to overcome the powerful pressures to treat the other as an object of annoyance, a nuisance to be neutralized or ignored. But the wonderful thing about an idea conversation is that the stakes are so small. As we have seen, no decision need be made. The only reason we are in an idea conversation is for our pleasure and learning. Even if it were necessary to sacrifice some of that pleasure and learning in order to treat the other lovingly, it seems like a small price to pay. My own sense is that far from degrading the potential for pleasure and learning that it contains, a loving idea conversation is the very best way to both learn and have a good time.

Remember the advice my parents gave me? They said, "Never discuss politics or religion." The idea was that I was sure to get into a very unpleasant squabble and maybe lose a friend in the process. This common notion says something about the way we were raised and educated, doesn't it? We were trained to overlook the possibility that it could be wonderfully instructive to have a friend whose religion or politics were different from ours. Perhaps she could teach us something new about her outlook and even learn something surprising about ours. Instead, we were locked into the idea that it's somehow necessary for us to argue about whether God has an opinion about birth control or eating pork. We act as though arguing for an idea and against a different idea is a matter of loyalty and integrity—and as though *not* arguing is the equivalent of recanting our religious or political or literary or artistic faith. We seem to believe that not arguing marks us as wishy-washy, as not firmly standing up for what we believe.

My position is that arguing about an idea precludes accepting and encountering the other person for whom he or she is. Arguing insists that the other person become, for now at least, identical with ourselves. When we make that demand, we are in what Buber called an I-It relationship.

4. None of us, not the very smartest or the very best informed, can see all the way to the end of the vastness. But when we argue, we seem to be claiming that we do. One of the hardest and at the same time most essential things for us to keep in mind is that our vision is limited, that there are more things in heaven and earth than are dreamt of in our philosophies. We will not be available to learn anything if we think we know it all already.

Paul Reps tells of the Zen master being questioned by a philosophy professor. The professor talked brilliantly and at length before asking his first question, and when he asked it the master responded by pouring a cup of tea until it began to overflow. The professor exclaimed that there was no room for more tea. The master smiled and said there was no room for more philosophy in the professor's head.

It is natural enough that we make the error of thinking we can see it all. My own perceptions give no very clear indication of their limitations. The tree that falls in the forest, out of my earshot, simply doesn't exist for me; nothing reminds me that something is going on over there that I have missed.

When put like this, it seems self-evident. We do in fact know that the telescope has not been built that can see Mars very well, let alone the details of a neighboring galaxy. I have barely mastered my own subspecialty in school, let alone all of the thousands of subjects I have not even read about. And of course I really know in my secret heart that I have not come anywhere near mastering even my subspecialty. The acknowledged *masters* in it have not come anywhere near mastering it. All of us are only beginning to wonder how to approach it.

Similarly with my view of you. I know how little I know of you. If I were to study you from now on, I would still know only an infinitesimal fraction of who and what you are. Similarly with politics. Similarly with religion and baseball and stereo components and martinis and art. Similarly with everything. The vast domain of the unknown seems self-evident.

And yet for some mysterious reason we seem to act much of the time as though we saw all the way to the ends of the vastness. We are constantly telling each other where it's at. Conversations in college classrooms are often filled with arguments about opinions. Conversations outside of classrooms do not seem any different. Magazines and books (including, I'm afraid, this one) confidently explain the universe to the reader.

A scientist will begin a lecture by cautioning her students that we do not ever know the truth, but only continue to approach it—and go on to scoff at a theory coming out of a rival laboratory. When she speaks of the limits of what she knows, she is acknowledging that her opinions merely generate hypotheses she hopes to test. But in conversation, she, like the rest of us, falls into the error of forgetting that and believing that her opinions describe the world the way it actually is.

The problem is not that we have opinions nor that we state them. Opinions are our way of organizing our current perceptions and sharing them with each other. The problem is the surprising ease with which we seem to forget that our opinions are only our *current* perceptions and send them off into battle as though they were revealed truth.

It is instructive to pause once in a while and remember how rigidly our upbringing, our culture, and our language have conditioned our perceptions and our opinions. The conditioning is easy to see in extreme cases. One's view of politics or religion is likely to be limited almost hopelessly by one's cultural context. So is one's view of LSD or the power of the rain dance or the place of women. The conditioning is harder to see in the more subtle cases, but it is no less powerful.

Alan Watts has eloquently shown how learning the language of the occident has shaped our world view. Our language of subjects and objects shows us a world in which you do things to me or I do them to you. Given a different cultural context and linguistic structure, we could view ourselves as part of flowing, interpenetrating systems in a world in which things "just happen."

When the ghost appears, Hamlet asks his mother, "Do you see nothing there?" She replies with a confidence embarrassingly reminiscent of us all, "Nothing at all; yet all there is I see." It seems very unlikely that she sees all there is. Even if the ghost is no more than the very coinage of Hamlet's brain, there is a good deal more in Gertrude's field of vision than she sees.

The deep woods guide sees far more than I along the trail we walk. I don't mean that he interprets it more richly, though indeed he does. I mean that I simply don't *see* things until he shows them to me. I don't see the faint animal tracks and almost hidden berries and the gradual change of the quality of the underbrush as we go from forest to chaparral. And still I feel the temptation to say, "All there is I see."

I look out the window to see if there's snow on the ground. If there is, that is all I see. My friend who is a skier looks and sees subtle variations of snow that I never noticed. The great linguistic anthropologist Benjamin Whorf tells us that the Eskimos have some sixteen words for snow, and this suggests that they look at the white-covered ground and see subtleties lost on even my sophisticated skier friend.

So I can walk along the forest trail and say to my guide, "All there is I see." Or I can say, "I'm sure I see only a tiny fragment of what is there; would you show me some of the rest?" It's not hard to remember to be this modest in the Maine woods, but very hard to remember when you and I are discussing a play or a book or a religious doctrine or a political issue.

Let me repeat that none of this is to say that opinions, beliefs, and judgments are not perfectly valuable things to have and to reveal. The fact of the matter is that we do have them, and it would be polite hypocrisy to pretend that we don't. The issue is how we treat them in conversation. If we treat them like battle standards to fight under, we are like the scientist who confuses a hypothesis with the whole of reality. But if we treat our opinions like signposts indicating how far into the subject we have seen so far, then a conversation need not be the clash of opinions.

When we remember, it seems clear and self-evident that none of us knows everything about anything. We are back in the Maine woods, on a journey toward ever-increasing richness of awareness. What I think about something now, what I know about something now, is only a temporary way station on that journey. It does not make any sense for me to tell you that I am right or you are wrong. How on earth do I know? All I know is that whatever I think now is only a temporary state of belief— and, that you may quite possibly be that guide to the Maine woods who will show me things not dreamt of in my philosophy. At the least, it is certain that I dream of fewer things in my philosophy than there are in heaven and earth. I will be far better off keeping an eye out for a glimpse of a new awareness than seizing every opportunity to ask you to take my temporary way station as your permanent abode. When I converse with the attitude that my opinion is the last word, I am trying to convert you to my truth. When I remember that I am not yet finished learning about this subject, then the conversation becomes a collaborative search for mutual enrichment. Since my view is by definition limited, I need every additional bit of vision I can get.

Not long ago I got into a conversation with a friend about the concept of sin and its usefulness in religious teaching. My friend believed that certain acts were sinful and that it was dishonest and dangerously misleading to teach anything else. Now reducing the amount of guilt in the world is a matter of paramount importance for me. My own guilt is a terrible burden in my life, and I have seen that guilt is a hardship for some of my clients and students and friends as well. Since teaching the concept of sin seemed a step in the wrong direction and I have some strong feelings on the subject, I began a sharp argument with her.

Then it slowly dawned on me that I was missing an opportunity to have my consciousness expanded. This was another human being with a whole different history and point of view, freed from all the narrowness my upbringing has bestowed on me. She had glimpses of the vastness not yet vouchsafed to me. And there I was, acting as though my temporary way station was where I was planning to live for the rest of my life. So I stopped arguing and joined her in exploring the usefulness of sin as an item of religious education.

It was a valuable conversation. I emerged excited by a new appreciation of the subject. My old point of view, i.e., that sin was nothing more than ancient theologians imposing their own guilt on me, was limited and narrow. As we explored this complex subject, new doors swung open for me. I had peeked a tiny bit farther into the vastness; so had she. I was not "converted"; many of my ideas still seemed useful to me. But I had now a broader view of the subject and more respect for people holding views that differ from mine.

Somewhere in that conversation, at the transition from argument to cooperative exploration, I had to face in myself the old accusation of being *wishy-washy.* Do I believe in my convictions or don't I? Do I stand up for what I believe or don't I? But the moment I start talking about "what I believe," I am acting as though I see all the way to the end of the vastness. Similarly, the phrases "I agree" and "I disagree" are helpful indicators of the current state of a developing viewpoint. But said dogmatically they contradict the fact that after all they only mean that my temporary way station is the same as or different from your temporary way station. My dogmatism is likely to convince me that I see all that there is to see. Thus the nobility of standing up for what I believe seems a pale return for having deprived myself of the opportunity to be shown some expanding new view of the vastness.

Let me remind you once more that all this depends on the distinction between a conversation in which a decision must be made and one in which there is no such need. Undoubtedly, the preliminary stages of a decision conversation would profit greatly from a generous, cooperative exploration of all available points of view. But however generous and cooperative the preliminary stages, mutually exclusive alternatives must eventually be recognized as such. I realize that when I finally have to make a decision or try hard to influence one, my view will always be finite and hopelessly incomplete, but when action is to be taken, my view is all I have. At that point, standing up for what I believe takes on a new meaning.

It is always liberating to remind ourselves that in an idea conversation no decision need be made.

A special form of limiting one's view is the *judging* of experience. Often we do not treat a movie or a book as something to be experienced, enjoyed, and learned from, but rather as something to be judged as good or bad. Actors sometimes say that the only time they get to play before an audience is when they play to kids. At all other times they are playing to a house full of critics who are less intent on experiencing the play than on forming judgments about the script and the actors and the scenery and the costumes, so as to arm themselves for the coming lobby-talk.

Often this is the result of having been raised in fear of being caught with the wrong judgment. Safety in such matters lies in finding fault with as much as possible. It is much easier to defend a negative judgment than a positive one. Better to look jaded and cynical than naïve and uninformed. Beethoven is sometimes chided by his biographers for having no discrimination in poetry. He could study and exult over his age's "sentimental trash" with the same passion he gave to Goethe and Shakespeare. Some of my students have confessed to me that they are ashamed to listen to some music which moves them because it is considered corny by their peers.

What Beethoven seems to have known is that it is very hard to have your mind expanded if you have to ask each guide who wanders by if he or she has received the fashion arbiter's seal of approval. It would be bad enough if we were restricted to enjoying only those who have received the seal. But it is even worse than that, because we are often so busy checking out the guide's credentials (Is this good or bad? Shall I praise it or condemn it? May I be found listening to it?) that even if the work gets a passing grade, our attention has been so preempted by the judgment process that there is very little room left to experience, enjoy, and learn from the experience.

As with all opinions, the problem lies not in having or revealing judgments. The problem comes when we sacrifice the experience of the play or the book to the formation of those judgments and when we sacrifice an interesting conversation to the defending of them.

Someone said to Harold Clurman, one of America's greatest theatrical directors, that one of his plays was very good. He is reported to have replied, "I don't care whether you thought it was good or bad; I only care that it changes your life."

5. We learn most and are most creative when we *play* with ideas, rather than struggle with them. Since the only reasons to have an idea conversation are pleasure and enrichment, there's no sense in making the process painful or unpleasant. Certainly some kids can get a lot of pleasure out of wrestling for fun. Similarly some adults can get pleasure out of a knockdown, drag-out argument without losing sight of the essential love and playfulness which informs the talk. But that kind of pleasure is rare; more commonly the argument quickly evolves into a serious struggle, and the fun is gone.

Play is what kids do when they wrestle. Another kind of play, as we have seen, is what musicians do. Remember the jam session?

The jam session is an interesting model for an idea conversation, one that adds a new dimension to our exploration. So far we have been looking at the value of talking about ideas without playing one-up, that is without trying to win, to be right, or to convince. The jam session goes beyond that and suggests that an idea conversation could be an opportunity for us to spark new ideas in each other, to stimulate and be stimulated, to collaborate on building an idea or a collection of ideas richer and more complete than any we could have thought out on our own. And it suggests that, as in the jam session, the path to that goal is listening carefully to each other's ideas and treating them with considerable respect.

Every now and then I get an idea (rarely, I confess). I would love a chance to converse with you in order to try out my idea. I would like to see what you do with my idea, how you play with it, what it looks like when it is enriched by your unique perspective. I would like to give you a chance to try out some of yours on me. If our ideas seem to clash, I would enjoy the challenge of seeing if we could together invent a comprehensive, superordinate idea that would hold both of ours and somehow harmonize them.

It seems to me that it's hard to find *any* reason for having an idea conversation other than to enjoy ourselves, to connect with each other, to enrich our mental life. That suggests there's no conceivable reason not to do it playfully.

None of this is to imply that we don't take our ideas seriously, that we are not invested in them, that they don't sometimes represent deeply held values. (The music in a jam session can express many different moods, from exhiliration to profound grief.) Playing with ideas does not mean treating them lightly or with disrespect. On the contrary, this kind of conversation requires us both to treat our own and each other's ideas with considerable respect. And it asks of us that we keep in mind that our idea is not the last word on the subject. We might consider that however precious a given idea might seem to us, there is another value which may be equally precious: the I-Thou relationship. My most cherished idea is not more important to me than treating you with loving respect.

4

Let Me Tell You What You're Doing Wrong

Relationship Conversations

"You're not really available to me. You cut me short when we're on the phone, You always have some-where else to go or something else to do. You really don't care about me."

"You're very demanding. You want too much.

You want me to be continually available without any regard for my life."

"You never help around the house. You never pick up after yourself. You act like I'm supposed to be your mother."

"You are so damned compulsive. You act like somebody is coming to inspect the place. We're not going to die if some dishtowel is out of place."

"Why did you tell him you'd do that? You know we have a full weekend."

"That's a nasty tone of voice. What *is* going on?"

"It is not a nasty tone of voice. I simply want to know why you made that date."

When there is conflict in a relationship, the first impulse is almost always to tell the other person what he or she is doing wrong. In relationship conversations, as in idea conversations, our addiction to right and wrong turns conversation into conflict, and the conflicts that result often appear unresolvable. It seems to the participants that it is the situation that is unresolvable and that the conversational impasse merely reflects the situation. However, just as there are ways of talking about ideas that are cooperative and harmonious, it turns out there are non-combative ways of talking about relationships as well.

Some fifty years ago a group of social scientists began to study this problem. Their research tool was and continues to be the sensitivity training group, or "T-group," an agendaless group in which people are encouraged to talk about their relationships with each other. Noticing what kind of talk leads to conflict and what kind to harmony, the scientists observed that there were a few clear and simple principles governing such conversations. It is the purpose of this chapter to show how those principles can be applied to our own relationship conversations.

We saw in an earlier chapter that it was important to distinguish between idea conversations and decision conversations. Similarly, a relationship conversation is by definition one in which no decision need be made. And the chief decision that need *not* be made is who is right.

In the examples above, each couple is beginning an energetic argument. Was it a nasty tone of voice or wasn't it? Is one partner a slob or is the other one a compulsive? Is one of these people a bad friend or is the other one unreasonably demanding? In all of these conversations there is little likelihood that either of the parties are going to listen to each other—except to the extent it's necessary to gather information for a counterattack. It is just about impossible to listen—*really* listen—if the issue is winning or losing. It is certainly impossible to listen sympathetically.

The question is this: can these conversations be converted into a form in which *both people are right and there is nothing to argue about?* If they can, it would mean that people could listen sympathetically to each other and sincerely acknowledge the other's position without in any way derogating their own. The principles that have emerged from the study of T-groups are designed to bring about this conversion.

All relationship conversations are not conflictful, of course. There are conversations in which one person is trying to express love and appreciation for another, conversations in which people are trying to communicate important experiences to each other, conversations in which one person is trying to understand the puzzling behavior of another, and so on. We will see that the same basic principles apply to all relationship conversations. No matter what the topic is, all such conversations are greatly facilitated by attention to these principles.

Some Thoughts About Feelings

Early in their research, the students of relationship conversations discovered that the central issue was the sharing of feelings. Do feelings muddy the clear water of rational discourse, or are they actually that which clears the water? It soon became apparent that people pay surprisingly little attention to this subject. In our culture, we seem to be remarkably confused about what constitutes a feeling and what constitutes some other internal event (such as an opinion or a judgment). This confusion is a serious hindrance to communication. We also seem to have a good deal of uncertainty about when it is appropriate to share feelings. Now some of these uncertainties and confusions are undoubtedly genuine, but some part of them turns out to be not question or confusion at all, but rather the expression of the needs of one-upmanship. We will see as we proceed that one of the main requirements for successful one-up play is the *concealment* of feelings. For that reason and others we will see, the understanding of the role of shared feelings in relationship conversations is at the center of our topic.

Psychologists define feeling (or *emotion* or *affect*) as the perception of arousal in those bodily systems controlled by the involuntary (autonomic) nervous system. Heartbeat, respiration, sweating, stomach sensations, salivation, and sexual activation are examples. When there is unusual action in one of these systems and no obvious physiological explanation (e.g., I just ran up the stairs), we perceive ourselves as having a feeling and assume that that feeling has something to do with events perceived externally (an uncaged lion) or internally (I just remembered I forgot to turn off the stove). If there is no bodily arousal, we tend not to think of ourselves as having a feeling. (I may think that you're preparing to hurt me, but if that thought is not accompanied by physical arousal I am unlikely to say that I feel afraid.)

Since our culture does not promote body awareness, members of it are much quicker to perceive the arousal connected with powerful emotions (strong fear or anger, for instance) than that connected with the more subtle ones (longing, or boredom, or joy). The arousal is nonetheless there and is almost certainly being noticed at some level of awareness when a person reports feeling an emotion.

Thus there is a class of internal events which we generally agree are called feelings and which are connected with bodily arousal. A partial list includes love, anger, excitement, fear, boredom, tenderness, desire, happiness, sadness, worry, hope, disgust, pity, longing, shame, guilt, embarrassment, suspicion, and so on.

On the other hand, the various manifestations of *thought* (belief, opinion, attitude) are not accompanied by physical arousal. As we proceed, it will be important always to distinguish feelings from thoughts and to remember that the two have different vocabularies. For example, if the words "I feel" are followed by the word "that," it is an almost sure sign that what follows will not be a feeling at all. Here "feel" is being used as a synonym for "think" or "believe." "I feel that we ought to have another meeting tomorrow" is an opinion. So is "I feel that you don't like me." Thoughts refer to events we generally agree include beliefs, opinions, attitudes, and judgments.

Sharing thoughts without feelings and sharing feelings are very different modes of communication. What the T-group workers discovered, and what communications specialists have confirmed ever since, is that an emotional component is always present in a relationship conversation. If the goal is to emerge one-up, then concealing the feelings and dealing in opinions and judgments is good strategy. If, on the other hand, the goal is contact and understanding, sharing the feelings is indispensable.

The freedom to express feelings depends on the assurance that they are value-free, that they deserve neither praise nor blame. Unlike my actions, I do not choose my feelings; they just happen. I am unlikely to give free expression to feelings unless I can be released from having to decide whether a given feeling is good or bad. Most of us were raised to believe something very different, that some feelings were indeed very bad and others were distinctly preferable. That belief is a hard one to unlearn, but unlearning it can provide a big relief: it's all right for me to feel whatever I feel, and it's all right for you to feel whatever you feel. The feelings are not good or bad; they simply are.

The key we found to idea conversations was the discovery that there was nothing to argue about. It is equally liberating to discover that the same thing is true in relationship conversations. The participants may be upset and angry, they may see the situation very differently, and they may also be (are *likely* to be) convinced that there is nothing to do but plunge into an argument—an argument that no one will win and that will leave them both feeling worse. Nonetheless, this chapter will propose that there is nothing to argue about.

This discovery opens new vistas for relationship conversations. To enter this sacred realm it is only necessary to understand the power of building the conversation around the expression of feelings. There is simply no way to argue about feelings.

Well, of course, that's not quite true, is it? If you tell me you're *not* angry, I could insist that you are, and we could argue about that. So one of the conditions for entering this realm is that we agree that each person gets to be the expert on her or his own feelings. If you tell me you're not angry, that becomes the authoritative word on the subject. I may be suspicious of your statement—but my suspicion simply becomes the authoritative word on *my* state. We agree that you are not angry (you are the expert) and that I am suspicious (I am the expert), and we have nothing to argue about. There is no implication that either of us (or anybody else) knows the abstract "truth" of the matter. What we each know for certain, and that is all we know, is what we feel. And now the way is open to further exploration of the situation.

What Gets in the Way?

As you might expect, this approach is harder than it looks. For one thing, psychoanalysis has penetrated our culture to the extent that most of us are aware that vast regions of feelings are unconscious, and this knowledge tempts us all to read each other's minds. After all, since your feelings are apt to be unconscious, I may be in a better position than you to tell you what you're really feeling. Yet, that argument looks suspiciously like a rationalization, because mind reading is one of the most powerful weapons in the one-up game. Not only does mind reading shift responsibility onto the other person, but it often does so in a way that is impossible to answer back (since if you deny the feeling, I can easily score a point about your defensiveness). For example:

> "The reason you don't want to go out with me is that you're threatened by me."
>> "That's not true; I'm not a bit threatened by you."
>> "You're so threatened you can't even admit it."

Other common examples:

"I think you're really angry at me."

"I feel you're starting to get tired of me."

"You may not think you love me, but. . ."

"I know you don't really want to see this movie."

Ironically, even though psychoanalysis has contributed some of this difficulty to the culture, it has also taught us the biggest danger of it: one of the most important defenses that Freud described was that of *projection*, which means attributing to another person a feeling that I want him or her to have. I may want you to feel this way because the feeling exists deep inside me and it's more comfortable for me to deal with it outside myself, or I may project it because having you feel this way would satisfy some need of mine. But I want the feeling badly enough to convince myself that it's there. Depth psychology teaches that we are thus flagrantly unreliable instruments for ascertaining other people's feelings.

Playing by the Rules

These concerns underlie the first two rules for a noncombative relationship conversation:

1. We will build the conversation around our feelings.

2. We will extend to each other the courtesy of assuming that each of us is the expert on his or her own feelings.

Let's take the example with which we opened this chapter:

"You're not really available to me. You cut me short when we're on the phone. You always have somewhere else to go or something else to do. You really don't care about me."

"You're very demanding. You want too much. You want me to be continually available without any regard for my life."

Although these people may well believe that they have begun to face their problem openly, a moment's inspection reveals that neither party has actually shared any feelings. Compare that with this conversation:

"I felt quite hurt yesterday when I called you and you didn't have time to talk to me. It seems to me that whenever I call you have somewhere else to go or something else to do. What I'm afraid of is that you really don't care about me."

"I do care about you. And it's true that I do get annoyed sometimes when you call and talk about yourself at such length. It makes me angry that you demand so much of our friendship. And it saddens me that you don't seem to care about me or about how busy I might be when you call."

The first example boils down to an argument about who is right, about who is doing the friendship right. It is an exchange of accusations. In the second exchange there is certainly pain, but there is no argument and no accusation. And without argument or accusation there is a significantly better chance that the pain can be dealt with constructively.

You might wonder where this conversation can go now—what, at this point, would be the most constructive way to improve the contact and understanding between these two people. In chapter 5 we will suggest that a crucial ingredient in a relationship conversation is *empathy*—expressing it as well as experiencing it. In that chapter we'll explore some directions that conversations like this one might take.

Recall the second of our earlier examples:

> "You never help around the house. You never pick up after yourself. You act like I'm supposed to be your mother."
>
> "You are so damned compulsive. You act like somebody is coming to inspect the place. We're not going to die if some dishtowel is out of place."

How is this conversation going to happen without accusation and argument?

> "I'm getting pretty angry about the amount of picking up after you that I do. I'm in a bind: it upsets me when the house is messy, and it makes me mad to clean up your stuff. I wish you'd take equal responsibility for our home."
>
> "Your concern about the place being so neat makes me nervous. I'd like to be able to relax in my own home without worrying about where I left the dishtowel."

Now the cards are on the table, and there is a place from which to start working this one out. It will still be necessary to make some decisions about how the house is to be kept, but an important first step has been made. The two people are learning each other's feelings and learning them in a way that leaves no opening for an argument. One person is angry and upset; the other is made nervous by the requirements of neatness. They are now in a position to acknowledge each other's feelings without the question of right and wrong being raised. And it may be presumed that if these people care about each other they will want to take this valuable information seriously. As in the previous example, considering the role of expressed empathy will help us understand where to go with this conversation.

Defensive Moves

As we proceed with this chapter, we will consider some refinements of emotion conversation developed by the T-group workers—refinements that will help the people in these painful conversations increase their understanding of each other and will optimize their chances of resolving the conflict. But before we go on to consider these principles, there is another topic to be explored: *defensiveness.* Defensiveness is the single most serious obstacle to straight talk and straight listening in relationship conversations.

Defensiveness is the refusal to hear and accept another's feelings about me. It is always a manifestation of the one-up game. When I am defensive I am making a clear statement that l am not presently willing or able to engage in straight talk. What I'm interested in is winning—or at least limiting my losses.

> A: I really don't like it when you make us late like this. I get nervous and feel guilty toward the people we're meeting.

> B: I'm doing the best I can. I had a lot to do and I had to make that phone call. And you're not perfect either.

B's response is certainly understandable. He believes he is being criticized, and defending oneself against criticism is a natural response. But defensiveness has two costs: it escalates the tension and it puts distance between the people. (Whether B was actually being criticized is an interesting question to which we will return.)

> A: You're scary to me sometimes. When you're quiet and withdrawn like this I get afraid that you're mad at me and are going to attack me.

> B: I'm really not a dangerous person. You don't understand me very well.

Now it's an interesting and important question whether A did or didn't call B a dangerous person. But whatever the answer to that question is, B has chosen to focus on the fact that A doesn't see him the way he sees himself. As we'll find in a moment, that's a costly choice.

A: I felt hurt when you said that.

B: That's your problem. I didn't mean to hurt you.
You're too sensitive.

Here A is playing communication and B is playing chess. B "wins," and communication is thoroughly blocked.

Note that in each of these three examples B sees it as being to his advantage to claim that A is wrong. B fears he is about to be one-down and tries to put A down in order to *defend* himself (thus illustrating the origin of the word *defensiveness*). An inspection of the conversations reveals that the issue of right and wrong was entirely introduced by B. Since A spoke only of his feelings, there is no actual implication of right and wrong; the issue is not raised. In the eyes of some cosmic judge, B might have been absolutely right to delay the departure to make the phone call, had perfectly benign intentions toward A, and had no intention whatsoever to hurt A.

A never claimed otherwise; he merely reported the feelings stirred in him by B's behaviors or manner. So though it is understandable that B believed he had been criticized by A and was being called a dangerous or insensitive person, in fact none of these things happened. A's statements of feeling say nothing about B, only about A himself. That is why in some communication systems statements like those that A made are called "I statements."

B's saying "That's your problem" is a form of defensive response that illuminates an important area of communication theory. A tells B his feeling ("I felt hurt when you said that"). B responds as though A had asked "Whose problem is it?" and answers the unasked question by ruling that the problem is A's.

But is A's feeling anybody's problem? This is another way of asking, "Which of the two is right and which wrong?" Is A a hypersensitive person who gets hurt too easily? Or is B, at least in this conversation, a hurtful person? Since the cosmic judge is not likely to speak to us, there is no possible answer to these questions. Such truth is simply not accessible to mortals.

The only *fact* we have is that A felt the way he felt. Trying to convert that fact into one or the other of them being right is a one-up move. If B is interested in interacting with A, A's feelings are important information for B to have. Similarly, B's feelings on hearing of A's hurt would be important for A to hear.

The issue of defensiveness also raises another important concept in communication theory: *intent* versus *impact*. The T-group workers point out that these two mental states are often not the same and that it can be extremely useful to distinguish between them. When B responds by saying "I didn't mean to hurt you. You're too sensitive," it might be perfectly true that B had no intention whatsoever to hurt A. B is *the* expert on his own intentions and can't be controverted. And B's knowledge of his intentions is important information for A to have. Similarly, only A can know the impact B has had on him; he is *the* expert. His description of the impact can no more be disputed than B's description of his intent. And it's clearly to B's advantage, and certainly to the advantage of the relationship, for B to learn about the impact he has had. Once this concept is grasped, there is something wonderfully relieving about discovering that *there is nothing to argue about*. Both people are perfectly right.

All of us are often tempted to be defensive, and just about everyone succumbs sometimes. There are two primary reasons for this:

1. Whether or not we are actually being criticized, we tend to keep a vigilant lookout for it. Hearing criticism, real or fancied, is often painful (and leaves us one-down), causing us to raise our defensive shield.

2. When we hear someone present an image of ourselves that clashes with our self-image, our understandable first response is to defend our picture of ourselves.

Let's see how the above three examples of defensiveness might have gone had B made the non-defensive choice.

A: I really don't like it when you make us late like this. I get nervous and feel guilty toward the people we're meeting.

B: I'm doing the best I can. I had a lot to do and I had to make that phone call. And you're not perfect either.

We've seen that B's (very understandable) defensiveness turns A's self-disclosure and attempt at contact into a struggle from which an improved connection between them is unlikely to emerge. Now let's suppose that B had opted not to defend himself, but to respond with his own feelings.

A: I really don't like it when you make us late like this. I get nervous and feel guilty toward the people we're meeting.

B: I know you do. I don't like making you feel that way. And I get a little bit irritated that you are so worried about it. It doesn't seem to me such a big deal.

Now the way is open for increased mutual understanding:

A: I know it doesn't seem important to you, and I think you're probably right that it's not a big deal. But just the same I can't help feeling nervous about keeping them waiting.

B: I appreciate your saying that. I really don't like making you nervous. And I suppose it wouldn't kill me to try to be on time once in a while.

In our next example, A began with an expression of fear.

A: You're scary to me sometimes. When you're quiet and withdrawn like this I get afraid that you're mad at me and are going to attack me.

B's defensive response was:

B: I'm really not a dangerous person. You don't understand me very well.

A very different exchange might have followed if B had acknowledged the feelings he had.

B: I feel bad that you get scared of me. Sometimes I just get myself isolated and can't reach out. It doesn't mean I'm angry. I want you to trust me, and it feels awful that you think I'm going to hurt you.

A: It's a relief to have you say that. Maybe you could tell me when you're feeling isolated so I don't get paranoid about it.

B: I really will try.

Here's how B responded in our third example, when A said, "I felt hurt when you said that."

B: That's your problem. I didn't mean to hurt you. You're too sensitive.

Again, a very different response might well have produced a very different exchange.

B: I'm sorry that hurt you. I really am. I don't like hurting you. But I don't like having to be so cautious around you. I feel boxed in by having to be so careful how I say things.

A: I don't like it either. I know I'm super-sensitive. What I'd like is for you to be however you are and just give me the space to tell you when I'm hurt.

B: That's generous. I appreciate your giving me that space. I wouldn't mind being a little careful.

It does seem clear, doesn't it, that if we can allow the defensive impulse to subside and offer our feelings instead, the chances for a loving connection are greatly improved.

We have now learned the basic principles of relationship conversations. Some further refinements can make such conversations more harmonious and more loving, even when the topic is difficult or painful.

Disclose First; Question Second

In a relationship conversation, the principles of straight talk suggest that I lay my cards on the table before I ask you to. This means that while asking questions may not be helpful, disclosing the feeling that *prompts* the question is always helpful.

A good model for what happens when we play one-up is the game of chess. In chess it is necessary that my opponent be kept in the dark about my strategy and that he be duped into committing himself before I do, hopefully committing himself into a disadvantageous position. New Yorkers used to acknowledge the pervasiveness of this strategy in daily life with the expression "Does Macy's tell Gimbel's?"

The one-up game has become so much a part of us that even when we are trying hard to disarm and make contact it rarely occurs to us to lay our cards on the table before we ask the other person to.

Sharing a feeling constitutes an act of openness; asking a question about another's feelings constitutes an (often unconscious) one-up ploy. Often the question emanates from and sometimes conceals a feeling of our own that could be expressed in the form of a statement.

This is a new way of conversing for most of us and is not easy to learn. We are not always eager to surrender the one-up advantage; also, even with the best will in the world, the long-standing habit of asking questions makes it hard to identify the feeling that prompted the question. The T-group workers found that once the concept of "feelings underlie questions" is grasped, this difficulty vanishes.

Let's look at some examples.

"How do you feel about Mary?"

This question seems innocent enough, and indeed it might well be. But let's look at the possibilities. If my question is all you have to go on, you don't know how *I* feel about Mary. If Mary is our boss and our workplace is factionalized, you may well want to know just exactly why I'm asking you that question before you answer.

"How are you feeling about the way you handled the meeting yesterday?"

It would take an awfully secure person to feel good about answering that question without more information—more secure than most of us are. Even if you felt pretty good about the meeting, you might well want to arm yourself against a possible impending criticism by criticizing yourself first.

"We've been friends for quite a while. I'd like to know if you're attracted to me as more than a friend."

This one is fraught with danger. Is it the introduction to a rejection? Is it a precaution taken by someone who doesn't want to expose his attraction first?

When you become aware of a question rising in you and have difficulty finding the generating feeling, there are three questions you can ask yourself:

1. Why am I asking this? (Idle curiosity is an inadequate answer, simply because toying with one's brothers and sisters is not good for communication.)

2. What answers would please me? (What am I *hoping* for?)

3. What answers would displease me? (What do I *fear?*)

Openness Means Taking Risks

Of course, the chief risk is that I could wind up one-down.

In our culture, maybe in all cultures, making genuine, loving contact is not always safe or easy. Believing that there are people around who want to hurt me is not paranoid—at least not entirely paranoid. This is in fact a one-up world. There is always a chance that the feelings I expose will be seen as an opening by someone looking for a one-up opportunity and that I could get hurt. This is one reason disarmament conferences are so unproductive. The never-ending fear is that one side will take advantage of the other's attempt to cooperate and launch an attack.

There is always a risk involved in trying to make a real connection. But without that risk, all we can hope for is a superficial contact or profitless struggle in which both people conceal important things from each other in the interests of staying safe.

At a business meeting Arthur finds himself being attacked and criticized, the attack being led by his colleague, Dick. At the end of the meeting, Arthur feels bewildered and angry—angry at everyone who attacked him, but mostly at Dick. It seems likely to him that his relationship with Dick has been permanently damaged. At home that night his phone rings.

Dick: Arthur, it's Dick. I'd like to talk to you if you've got a few minutes.

Arthur: Okay.

Dick: I was telling Nancy what happened today, and she got upset and asked me what the hell I was up to. We talked for a while, and I realized some things that I want to tell you. This is hard for me to say.

Arthur: What is, Dick?

Dick: Arthur, I think I'm actually very competitive with you. I think I'm jealous of how much Bill admires you. I think what happened today was that I saw a chance to make you look bad and to score some points over you and I went for it. I think it was a crappy thing to do, and I'm really sorry you took such a beating in there today. There's no way you deserved that.

This is a very gutsy thing for Dick to have done—and a very risky one. Not only does he put himself at serious disadvantage in his competition with Arthur, but he exposes himself to the possibility of hurtful gossip. He is running a significant risk. Yet there is also a large payoff. He has protected his relationship with Arthur, which was in real danger, and he has earned the incomparable satisfaction of feeling, at least for this evening, like an honest person. Of course there is the danger that Arthur will use his admission against him at some future time. But there is also a real chance that he has earned Arthur's trust and made him into a friend and ally.

There are two possible bases for this kind of risk taking. The first is that Dick trusts Arthur not to take advantage of his openness. The second is that Dick has decided that, whatever the risk, he can live more easily with himself (and perhaps with Nancy!) if he plays straight with Arthur. Whatever Arthur chooses to do with this information, Dick has his own conscience to deal with. Another way of saying this is that Dick has found that there are things more important to him than his one-up score.

The ultimate extension of this position is to stop paying attention to the scoreboard altogether. Such a person might figure: "If I get hurt, I get hurt. No matter, I'll just go on trying to identify and reveal my feelings." This position gives one ultimate security since it doesn't depend on the good will of the other person. It is also very hard to attain, since the laws of the one-up game are ubiquitous and are deeply embedded in each of us. But with the persons close to us, the people with whom we live and work, the cost of defensiveness is so high and the rewards of risk taking so great that it pays to gamble. The truth is, as we all know at some level, there isn't *really* that much to lose anyway.

An issue came up in the conversation between Dick and Arthur that we will explore in chapter 6: the issue of atonement. Dick said to Arthur: "I think it was a crappy thing to do, and I'm really sorry you took such a beating in there today. There's no way you deserved that." The offer of atonement in that statement is found in "I'm really sorry. . ." Atonement and its value are not something our culture knows much about, and it's very costly that we don't. It is a topic worthy of our attention, and we will examine it at some length.

Reward the Risks Others Take

A person interested in developing the capacity for communication and contact can never be sure that his or her openness will not be taken advantage of. But that person can be careful never to use the openness of another to score points.

In the above example, Dick has made himself very vulnerable to Arthur by his courageous and generous admission. It is a delicate moment in their relationship. If Arthur responds with an attack (for instance: "I'm glad you've finally seen how competitive your are, Dick"), that is almost certainly the last time Dick will be this generous toward him. In fact, it may be a long time before Dick risks being generous to anybody. But if Arthur can meet generosity with generosity ("I really appreciate your calling me, Dick, and I also appreciate your being willing to take responsibility for the scene at the office. Thank you"), two things have happened: their relationship has been significantly improved, and Dick is more likely to risk generosity in the future. Psychologists refer to this phenomenon as the theory of *reinforcement*. If a behavior is "reinforced," i.e., rewarded, it is more likely to occur again.

Don't Lose Sight of Compassion

When being open and truthful, it is important to remember that the goal is not just to tell the truth and let the chips fall where they may. The goal is to tell the truth in such a way that the other person can receive it and to tell it in a context of compassion for the receiver.

Some 25 years ago the "encounter group" movement in California experimented with *truth-at-all-costs*. The idea was that those of us with a typical middle class upbringing had been strangled by the rules of politeness. Those workers thought the cure would be to encourage unmodulated truth and to let the receivers take care of themselves. To many who participated in that experiment, although the freeing of expressiveness certainly had value, the resulting interactions often seemed heartless and destructive. For people whose goal was more loving contact, this was not the path.

To follow the single criterion of truth is no doubt easier than to ask myself to find a way of saying the truth compassionately. Nonetheless, it seems essential that I do ask this of myself.

Sally and Paul are dressing to go out with friends. Sally finishes dressing and turns to Paul for appraisal.

> *Paul:*   I would be really embarrassed to be seen with you wearing all that makeup.

Sally, in tears, cancels their plans on the spot. The evening is in ruins.

Paul stayed with our major principle: he said his feelings. He didn't call her tasteless, and he didn't ask her a trap question. And still he hurt her badly.

This is a very tricky situation. There's no way that Sally is going to feel wonderful about Paul not liking her makeup. And certainly Paul does have the option of deciding that expressing his feelings is not worth the pain they will cause and keeping his mouth shut. There are undoubtedly times when discretion is the better part of valor. But this is not one of those. This is a topic of sufficient importance to Paul that he needs to address it.

What other choice does he have? Is there a way to get his message across and still protect Sally? Or at least to protect her as much as possible?

Let's try Sally and Paul's scene again.

Sally and Paul are dressing to go out with friends. Sally finishes dressing and turns to Paul for appraisal.

> *Paul:*   Do you really want my opinion?

Sally: Yes, I really do.

Paul: I love the dress, and you look really good in it, but to tell you the truth I really don't love the makeup.

Sally: What's wrong with the makeup?

Paul: There may be nothing wrong with it, Sal. It's just a bit heavier than I like, and it makes me feel a bit uncomfortable. If you wouldn't mind, I would be really grateful if you'd tone it down a bit.

"Embarrassed" and "uncomfortable" aren't quite synonymous here, but the message is conveyed nonetheless. In both examples, Paul has told the truth. In the second he has done his best to honor his love and concern for Sally without sacrificing his truth. It's by no means certain that the second version will have an altogether smooth outcome, but the chances are greatly improved.

Those, then, are the principles of relationship conversations that have emerged from the study of the T-group:

- We share our feelings.

- We extend to everyone the courtesy of being the expert on their own feelings.

- We are vigilant against our own defensiveness.

- We lay our own cards on the table before we ask the other to do so.

- We are willing to take risks.

- We reward risk taking in the other person.

- We try hard not lose sight of our compassion.

The next two chapters will refine our view of relationship conversation by examining the concept of *empathy* and looking at the seldom considered topic of *atonement*.

5

We Had Spaghetti Three Times Last Week

Empathy

The material we explored in the chapters on idea conversations came to us from the study of college seminars. The material in the last chapter on relationship conversations was based on the study of T-groups. The material in this chapter comes from a source different from either of those: from the practice of psychotherapy.

Psychotherapists have been concerned with the topic of empathy since the profession began. They define empathy as the process whereby I make such complete connection with your feelings that I actually *experience* them, although at a lesser intensity. You can see why empathy has always been so important to therapists: it is the way they grasp the emotional experience of their clients.

In the 1940s, the psychologist Carl Rogers wrote that empathy was one of the attributes necessary for successful therapy. Twenty years later, the psychoanalyst Heinz Kohut went on to emphasize the importance of *communicating* that empathy to the client. He taught that it was essential for clients to be continually aware of the therapist's attempts to grasp their experience.

I would like to suggest that Kohut's point is not only applicable to psychotherapy. It is very important in *all* relationships that the other person be aware of our attempts to grasp his or her experience. We all have a basic human need to be seen, to be heard, to be understood. When I think I am understood, I feel connected. When I'm not understood, I feel isolated and lonely.

One of the most common complaints heard by couples' therapists is "He (or she) doesn't try to *hear* me."

In a relationship conversation, particularly one in which emotions are becoming intense, I am apt to focus on my own point of view and my own feelings, to the point of disregarding yours or at least seeming to disregard them. My inattention is likely to cause you to try harder to convey your feelings to me, thus causing me to try harder to . . . You get the idea.

Mary: Jean, I feel hurt and angry that you didn't come to my party. It was really important to me.

Jean: I know it was. The truth is I feel good about deciding to be with my son. It was the right decision for me, and I'm finally getting to be able to take care of my own needs.

Mary: Well, I was hurt, and I'm still hurt.

This is a tricky situation. Both people are playing by the guidelines described in the previous chapters. They are telling the truth and talking about their feelings. So both are indeed expressing themselves. Yet it still doesn't look like a wonderful place they're in. What's missing?

What's missing is that each believes that the other is solely concerned with her own feelings. Mary would like to know that Jean has heard her and cares about her pain. Jean would like to know that Mary has heard her and understands how important her newly won integrity is to her. Even though these two do indeed care about each other, the problem is that each fears she will be giving up her truth if she acknowledges the other person's truth. It has not yet occurred to them that they can do both—that there is no conflict.

Just Being Heard

Before we see how Mary and Jean might have dealt with their situation, I'd like to tell you a little about one of Kohut's psychotherapy principles. Kohut teaches that it is impossible for a therapist to fill all of a client's needs. In fact, filling all of a client's needs is probably undesirable as well. What is possible (and highly desirable) is for the therapist to fully *grasp* the client's need and openly empathize with it. And just as it is desirable to grasp the client's *need*, it is equally desirable to grasp and empathize with the client's *feelings*. Kohut teaches that one of the great unsatisfied hungers that most of us carry from our early days is just being heard, just having someone show us that they care enough to grasp what we are feeling.

Also most of us are raised to suspect that we have the wrong feelings. Many of our sexual feelings, our angry feelings, our jealousy, our envy, and countless other emotions are apt to have been proscribed. We live in the painful bind of having no control over these feelings that we suspect are bad. And we are used to having people tell us they are bad. If we were not told the feeling was bad, we are still likely to have been told, however gently, that it was the wrong feeling and that we would be better off with a different one. Similarly, when a need could not be satisfied, we might have been told that it was the wrong need and that we should drop it.

Ten-year-old Susan has just come home from school and is near tears.

Susan: Janet was really mean to me. She likes Jessica better than me now.

Mother: Honey, you shouldn't let things like that get you so upset. You know how kids are. Tomorrow she'll like you better again.

Mother's motives are loving and concerned. She wants to shield her daughter from the pain of other children's cruelty and to educate her for the inevitable troubles ahead. Yet, however pure Mother's motives are, it is not a good idea for her to teach her child that her feelings are wrong.

Exchanges like this are why so many of us grow up hungry to be heard, to have someone say "I really know how painful it is to have a friend turn away from you like that." These words will not bring Janet back. They may not even ease the pain of losing her. But they will give Susan something very precious—the gift of empathy.

Having someone show us that they are trying hard to grasp what we are feeling can provide great comfort—and a great boost to our self-esteem. Not the least of this comfort is discovering that someone cares enough about us to try to grasp what we are feeling. And, very importantly, the act of trying to grasp it implies acceptance.

Since few of us—maybe none of us—received enough empathy, we grow up with a strong need for it. Often the experience of receiving empathy is so unfamiliar that we can't even tell ourselves what it is we need. But we need it nonetheless—and we need it a lot.

Although it's easy to see how Kohut's ideas about empathy apply to our relationship conversations, it's not always so easy to let others know that we have heard and understood their feelings. If I am angry or hurt, it may take a lot of discipline for me just to tell you my own feelings instead of attacking you. It takes even more self-control and compassion for me to empathize with your feelings before I tell you mine. Sometimes it will be just too hard, and I will simply have to get my own hurt or angry feelings off my chest before I can even think about empathy. If the feelings are very strong, I may have to omit the empathy altogether. Yet much of the time, if I remind myself, I will be able to empathize with your feelings as well as tell you mine.

Perhaps we should think of empathy as the relationship conversation version of building the other person's barn.

Recall Mary and Jean's conversation earlier in this chapter:

Mary: Jean, I feel hurt and angry that you didn't come to my party. It was really important to me.

Jean: I know it was. The truth is I feel good about deciding to be with my son. It was the right decision for me, and I'm finally getting to be able to take care of my own needs.

Mary: Well, I was hurt, and I'm still hurt.

We observed that it seems likely that each fears that she will be giving up her own truth if she acknowledges the other's truth. But suppose the conversation went like this:

Mary: Jean, I feel hurt and angry that you didn't come to my party. It was really important to me.

Jean: I know it was. I do really hear that my not coming hurt you, and I want you to know that I can really understand that. I do understand how important that party was to you.

Mary: It really was, Jean, and it did hurt me that you didn't come.

Jean: It was a conflict for me because I do care about you. And I must tell you that though I had no wish at all to hurt you, I do feel good about deciding to be with my

son. It was the right decision for me; I'm finally
getting to be able to take care of my own needs.

Mary: I can understand that. I still feel hurt. I wish my party
had been more important to you. But I do get it that
you're learning to take better care of yourself and that
that's important.

This is only the beginning of this conversation. If these are
friends and if they care about their relationship, there is more to
be explored here.

What Do We Have to Lose?

Throughout this book we have taken the position that in a surprising number of conversations there is nothing to argue about.
Your opinion may be different from mine, your emotional response to a situation may be different from mine, your feelings
may not please me—and nonetheless neither of us is wrong.
That same premise makes it possible for us to empathize with
each other without giving up our truth.

It's easy to understand why we fear that empathizing
means selling ourself out. Some of us were raised in ways that
made other people's outlooks and feelings much more important than our own.

*One of Caroline's earliest memories is an afternoon when she was
having a really good time, only to be told that she was making too
much noise and disturbing her mother. She remembers countless other
times when she was told that her opinions about movies or clothes or
people were "wrong." Once she was angry with a friend, and her
mother told her that she was being hurtful to treat someone she cared
about so badly. She learned the lesson that her mother's feelings were
more important than her own, that everyone's feelings and opinions
were more important than hers. Eventually she got tired of that kind of
self-abnegation and began to claim the right to her own response.
Here's a conversation she had with her lover as a young adult.*

Caroline: I want to go to Europe by myself for a month this summer.

Art: That makes me feel terrible, Caroline. If you want to do your vacation without me, you must not care about me very much.

This is familiar territory for Caroline. She's still struggling with the old conditioning. She's not going to give into it, but she's still struggling with it. And so the idea of acknowledging Art's feelings feels very dangerous. It feels like the first step on the slippery slope to giving herself away. We can certainly empathize with her fear and understand why she might choose to respond stubbornly or even combatively. But, as we saw with Mary and Jean, empathy need not be that slippery slope. There is no essential contradiction between empathizing and remaining true to oneself. So, should the spirit of Dr. Kohut descend onto her shoulder and whisper into her ear, Caroline might say:

Caroline: Honey, I understand that. I know you'll miss me; I'll miss you too. I know it's threatening to have me go off by myself like that. I can really see why it upsets you. I hate making you feel bad. But I really want to do this trip.

And if Art gets the message he might reply:

Art: I know. I know how important it is to you to have that kind of experience on your own. I really do know how essential your independence is to you. But I really hate it. I worry about your safety, and most of all I worry about you meeting someone else.

This conversation has a long way to go. But the tone is clear. These are two people managing both to stand by their truth and to do their best to hear the truth of the other.

Let's look at a couple of other examples.

Anne, the head of the department has chosen Fred to conduct a training session. Fred's colleague, Sam, is miffed at not having been chosen.

> *Sam:* Anne, I have a lot of seniority over Fred, and I know this stuff at least as well as he does. What gives?
>
> *Anne:* You're not as good a teacher as he is. You're a no-nonsense engineer, and you intimidate people. And you can be pretty impatient.
>
> *Sam:* I really don't think I'm as bad as all that. I did a good job in the Los Angeles meeting.
>
> *Anne:* I'm sorry, Sam; I just don't think this is a job for you.

Anne is doing what she has to do. Let's replay this and see if a little empathy would take some of the sting out of it for Sam. In addition to wanting to avoid causing him unnecessary pain, Anne has an organizational stake in his morale.

> *Sam:* Anne, I have a lot of seniority over Fred, and I know this stuff at least as well as he does. What gives?
>
> *Anne:* Sam, I know you enjoy doing training, and I can really understand your getting upset over my giving Fred that assignment. I know that it feels bad, and I'm really sorry. There are things you do really well, but I don't think this is one of them.

Anne can then go on to tell Sam her concerns about him. Although her empathy may not make him ecstatic about being passed over, however no-nonsense an engineer he might be, it is still likely to be important to him that his boss does indeed care about his feelings.

Robert and Karen are honeymooning at a resort hotel. Karen is very much in love and enjoying acting like a honeymooner in public. Robert is becoming embarrassed by Karen's public displays of affection.

> *Robert:* Karen, I feel bad asking you this, but sometimes I get embarrassed when you hug me or kiss me a lot when there are other people around.
>
> *Karen:* (badly wounded) That makes me want to cry. I feel awful. It scares me that I've married a man who doesn't love me. And it makes me really mad that

you care more about what people think than you care about me.

Robert: That makes *me* mad. You can't care about *me* very much if my feelings aren't important to you.

We could imagine some pretty dangerous conversations that this situation could produce. Robert and Karen have chosen one of the most benign options, one in which they are bravely trying to respect the rules of relationship conversation by talking about their feelings. Now, suppose that they too had been in touch with the empathy muse and very much wanted to empathize with each other. Even for people who have very good will toward each other, this is a difficult situation. How is this couple to empathize with each other without denying themselves the expression of strong feelings? It seems likely that the feelings are so preemptory that they must be expressed before there is any room for empathy.

Robert: Karen, I feel bad asking you this, but sometimes I get embarrassed when you hug me or kiss me a lot when there are other people around.

Karen: *(badly wounded)* That makes me want to cry. I feel awful. It scares me that I've married a man who doesn't love me. And it makes me really mad that you care more about what people think than you care about me.

Robert: That makes *me* mad. You can't care about *me* very much if my feelings aren't important to you.

Karen: Robert, your feelings *are* important to me. I know you were raised to be embarrassed by any display of emotion, and I can see that it's worse when it seems very public to you. But it hurts me a lot when all of that is more important to you than our love for each other.

Robert: I know it does. I'm really sorry to hurt you, and I didn't want to say anything about it. But the embarrassment gets so strong that I can't control it.

Karen: I can really understand that.

Robert: And I can really understand you wanting to be
            affectionate with me without worrying about who's
            watching. I could even imagine you're proud of our
            being newlyweds and kind of like people seeing it. I
            can understand that.

This still leaves them to figure out what to do about public
displays of affection, but at least each has the assurance that the
other cares enough to try to understand. That assurance ought
to significantly improve the climate for the rest of the conversation.

*Bob and Elizabeth are in the software business. He is in charge of
new product development, and she is a sales manager.*

Elizabeth: Are you guys aware that you released the 920-3
              package long before it was really ready? Our
              customers are screaming. Not one of those has
              been trouble-free.

Bob: Don't yell at me. We were under orders to get it out
              by the first of the month. We had no choice.

Elizabeth: I don't see the virtue in putting it out if it's just
              going to come back at us. We're going to start
              losing customers. This is serious stuff we're
              talking about.

Bob: I don't know why you're getting on me. Talk to
              Helen. Talk to Wendell. I didn't make up that date.

Elizabeth: Why on earth do you accept a release date that you
              know you can't make?

Bob: Elizabeth, you know how this place works as well
              as I do. I don't "accept" anything. Nobody *asks* me
              if I can do it by the first of the month. I'm *told* to
              release it then.

Elizabeth: All I know is that you're the product-development
              department and the products aren't being devel-
              oped and it's likely to cost me my job.

Here are a couple of people under stress that neither of them can control. However much these two might be paid, they are not having an easy time of it. A little empathy would make life easier.

Elizabeth: Are you guys aware that you released the 920-3 package long before it was really ready? Our customers are screaming. Not one of those has been trouble-free.

Bob: I know. I'm really sorry. It has bugs in it, and I know that gives you folks a really bad time. There's nothing I could do about it. We were under orders to get it out by the first of the month. We had no choice.

Elizabeth: I don't see the virtue in putting it out if it's just going to come back at us. We're going to start losing customers. This is serious stuff we're talking about.

Bob: Elizabeth, I know. I feel as bad about it as you do.

Elizabeth: Yeah, I know. It can't be any fun for you guys to be forced to release a package that you know is going to come back at you. It's not fun for us either.

Bob: I know it's not. It's terrible for you people.

Elizabeth: Maybe you and I should go to Wendell together and try to talk some sense into him. Not that it would do any good.

Bob: *(with a wry laugh)* Not that it would.

The actual situation is no better than it was, but empathy has changed the climate. In fact, there is no real issue between these two; they both have to deal with a difficult policy from above. But their lives will certainly be more pleasant if they stay sympathetic with each other.

And If There Is No Conflict?

From the examples chosen for this chapter you will have noticed that the expression of empathy is most appropriate and valuable when there has been some conflict, pain, or unhappiness expressed in the conversation. It is not often appropriate at other times.

> *Jean:*   Mary, I've managed to rearrange my schedule. I'm coming to your party, and I'm really looking forward to it.

> *Mary:*   Jean, that makes me so happy. I'm really glad you're coming.

Jean may want to go on to say that she's pleased her presence is important to Mary, but there is clearly no need for her to empathize with Mary's happiness.

Occasionally, however, empathy may be appropriate in a non-conflict situation.

> *Susan is ten years old and bubbling with excitement.*

> *Susan:*   Mother, I got an A on the project!

> *Mother:*   I know how happy that must make you. You worked so hard on it.

That Reminds Me . . .

One issue remains. In a classic *Peanuts* strip, Charlie Brown pours out the pain of his heart to Lucy as they lean on the ever-present brick wall, gazing into space. He pours it out for three frames. In the last frame Lucy, gazing thoughtfully ahead, says, "We had spaghetti at our house three times this week."

Most of us are a little better at empathy than that, but there is a lesson there for all of us. It's good to remember how much each of us needs to be heard and responded to. Although, unlike Lucy, we are usually too sensitive to completely ignore the other person, we do sometimes tend to shortchange them. A common reason for this is that what they have said reminds us of something important of our own.

> *Paul:*   You look sad. What's happening?

Karen: It's the anniversary of my mother's death. I was missing her.

Paul: I think about my mother a lot too. She would have been sixty this year. I'm sorry the kids never really knew her.

Karen: I am too. I know you miss her a lot.

Paul's blunder is not a terrible gaffe, and it's a very understandable one. But even though it was not Paul's intent to do so, his words do leave Karen with the message that empathy is her job, not his. It is always worthwhile to keep in mind the value of giving the other person a full response before changing the subject, however slightly.

Openly empathizing, then, is a way of saying that no matter what you are feeling I am willing and able to grasp it and acknowledge it. Empathizing doesn't mean I feel the same way you do. It doesn't mean that your feeling pleases me or that I am prepared to deny my own feelings. It only means that you are important enough to me and that I care about you enough to do my best to hear you. That's all it means, but that is a great deal. And it is something all of us need.

6

How Do We Get *Out* of Trouble?

Atonement

Before we leave the topic of relationship conversations, there is one more issue to be addressed: getting out of trouble when one person has wronged the other.

Every relationship is recurrently in trouble. In that respect, one relationship is pretty much like another. What distinguishes them is what happens next. The secret of a good relationship may not be how well it avoids trouble, but rather how skillfully it gets out of trouble once it starts.

The particular kind of trouble to be addressed here occurs when one member of a relationship wrongs the other, and the wronged party emerges from the incident experiencing feelings that are bound to plunge the relationship into discord. Even in the most loving relationship imaginable, events like this are bound to happen at least once in a while.

John and Shirley are married. At a party, John, with a couple of drinks in him, begins kidding Shirley. The kidding escalates until John reveals a family secret that is considerably humiliating to Shirley. Later, at home, he tries to initiate affectionate contact. Shirley is having none of it. The relationship is in trouble.

Business and professional relationships have their moments of discord too.

Art and Chuck work for companies that do business with each other. Their job includes handling the communications between the two companies, and they talk regularly by telephone. Here is one of their conversations:

Art: Chuck, you promised to get the specs on the Foray project and send them to us. That was two weeks ago. What gives?

Chuck: Oh, I don't think so. Don't you remember? You said you would be talking to the Acme people, and you would get the specs.

Art: Dammit, Chuck, that's not true. I'm sure we agreed you would get them. And now Max wants to know where the hell they are, and I'm in trouble. And I don't like you pushing the responsibility off on me.

Chuck: Get off of me, Art. I'll call Acme and get the damned specs. If you want to know, I think I've got a fax in the files confirming that you agreed to do it. You might check your own files too.

The files in both offices confirm Chuck's memory. Art had indeed agreed to do it. Chuck faxes the specs to Art and phones him.

Chuck: Did you get the specs?

Art: Yeah, I did; thanks.

Chuck: Did you check your file?

Art: Yeah, I did.

Chuck: Well?

Art: Well, what?

Chuck: Well, whose screw-up was it?

Art: *(after a pause)* Yeah, I'd agreed to do it.

There's a long pause.

Chuck: Okay, I'll talk to you later.

Art: So long.

Business is business, and these men will continue to work together, but the relationship has been damaged, and the damage is likely to show up some day.

Mark and Kathy are college students who live together. They have agreed that their relationship does not have to be a monogamous one. Mark spends a night with their friend, Liz, and, true to their contract, tells Kathy about it—in considerable detail. They discuss the episode a good deal, and each time they do Mark once again recounts the positive nature of the experience. Each time they discuss it, Kathy says how hurt and jealous she is, particularly by Mark continuing to pile it on. Finally they decide that an open relationship is too difficult, and they agree to try monogamy. After a time, Kathy spends the night with their friend, Bob, and tells Mark about it—in considerable detail. The relationship is in serious trouble. In fact, it was never out of trouble since Mark slept with Liz.

Let's begin by agreeing that the continuing difficulty in all these incidents is *not* that one partner has wounded the other.

By malice or by accident or by the intricate complexities of the connections between human beings, such wounding is inevitable. It happens in all significant relationships, and it happens with some frequency. The difficulty is that once the wounding has occurred, our culture provides no real way out.

Is there a way out? Let's see if we can find one.

Not-So-Sweet Revenge

The wronged party in situations like these faces two problems. First, he or she must certainly experience some increased expectation of being wronged again and therefore a decrease of trust. Both people are likely to be aware of this problem, concerned about it, and puzzled by their inability to deal with it.

The second problem is one they are likely to find more difficult to label, since it is apt to include some protective self-deception. This problem will come as no surprise to a reader who has gotten this far in this book: the wronged person is likely to be filled with resentment over the injustice and to feel one-down. Thus our wronged party is likely to feel the hurt, shame, jealously, or anger that go with seeing oneself as betrayed or humiliated. And somewhere, buried deep or lying shallow in every one-down breast, is the thirst for revenge. No relationship is likely to do well while one of the people is in this state.

The need for revenge presents three options.

(1) You can bide your time, pick your spot, and strike back. The consequences of striking back are predictable: the seesaw has merely tilted, and now the other partner starts biding his or her time.

(2) You can live on at slow boil, the matter increasingly submerged by time, but nonetheless fueling a continuing low-grade anger and mistrust. As incident after incident of this kind piles up, the relationship steadily deteriorates.

(3) You can simply leave the field. The thirst for revenge remains unsatisfied (out of fear or moral scruple), the trust in

the other person's caring and honor decreases to an unacceptably low point, and the relationship becomes just too painful. At that point, the wronged person is apt to sever relations.

Dealing with one-down feelings is very difficult because acknowledging being one-down seems even more humiliating. As a result, it's hard for us to admit such feelings even to ourselves.

So the situation now looks like this: I have wronged you. You are (perhaps a little, perhaps a lot) hurt, angry, betrayed, humiliated. Your trust in me has plummeted, and you are thirsting to even the one-up score—that is, you need revenge. You are unlikely to acknowledge this need for revenge because it's uncool: it puts you down another notch. And what if you were to acknowledge your situation and ask my help in liberating you from it? I wouldn't know what to do about it however much I might want to help.

I might promise not to do it again. You would have no reason to doubt my good intentions, and yet you feel unsatisfied. It's not hard to understand why (and I would like to emphasize this): *your one-down feelings are not being dealt with.* Their very presence is blocking our attempts to raise the level of trust, so it's understandable that you are not fully confident I won't hurt you again.

We are caught in the net of resented injustice with no exit in sight. It's a common situation, and there seems to be no culturally acceptable way out.

The Lost Language of Atonement

In these situations the two people have lost an existing harmony through some (at least perceived) transgression of one partner. In the language of medieval England, they were formerly "at one," are now "at variance," and need to be "at-oned" again. Our own language stores a memory of that "at one" state in the verb "atone." Though our own culture may not provide a way of doing it, it recognizes that atonement is what is needed.

The word *atonement* has come down to us with two meanings. It means *becoming one,* and it also means *making amends.* In the situations we have been examining, both meanings are relevant. Certainly reconciliation and a return to oneness is the goal, and it looks as though, in order to attain it, the offending person is somehow going to have to make amends and square the offense.

This problem of atonement is what we're concerned with in this chapter. I have wronged you. I need to square that wrong somehow and provide us a way back to "at-onement." But our culture provides no such way.

In fact, our culture seems to go out of its way to make atonement difficult. I learned a great deal about this difficulty when I used to conduct workshops for couples. As part of the workshop, I hoped to help the couples clean out past resentments and also to provide them with a way of dealing with future ones. And so I designed an atonement ritual. I confess I did not anticipate how many cultural obstacles would need to be surmounted before the couples could fully give themselves to the ritual.

The essence of the ritual was that one partner would express all the stored resentments and bad feelings that he or she had. Then the other partner would take some time to think all this over and examine his or her heart to see what parts of the list did indeed seem to be a transgression about which he or she felt bad.

Here's how John might respond to Shirley's feeling of injury.

> John: There's a lot that you said that I'm feeling terrible about. I'd like to start with the party at the Wilsons'. Talking about your phobia in public that way, just to razz you, was a really crummy thing to do, and I feel awful about it. Honey, I'm really sorry. I apologize to you and I ask you to forgive me, if you can, for humiliating you so.

The ritual's ground rules give Shirley three options. She can ask for more information; she can say, "Sorry, I'm still too mad, but I hope you'll ask me again sometime"; or she can accept the atonement. In that case she says, "Thank you for the apology. I do forgive you and I'm ready to let it go."

Here's an exchange between Mark and Kathy.

> *Mark:* Kathy, all the trouble we've had really starts with my sleeping with Liz. We thought it would work okay for us to sleep with other people, and we were wrong. And I could have been a lot more sensitive about the way I talked to you about it. I was really hurt by your sleeping with Bob, but I can understand how mad you were at me. I want to apologize to you, both for sleeping with Liz and for the way I talked about it. I'm really sorry, and I would like to ask you to forgive me.

> *Kathy:* (*embracing him*) Thanks. I do forgive you, of course. I really appreciate the apology. I have a lot to apologize for too. For not standing by our contract, for not asking you to stop when the story was getting so painful, and most of all for sleeping with Bob when we had agreed we wouldn't do things like that. I am really sorry for all of that. I apologize and ask you to forgive me.

In this way, the cycle of humiliation and revenge is broken.

A Sense of Release

When this ritual was first suggested to the members of the workshop, many responded with embarrassment and some anxiety. They felt uncomfortable about their partner apologizing, about apologizing themselves, and about giving themselves the right to forgive.

Once able to work through this distaste, the couples did find a willingness in themselves to introduce these archaic concepts of apology and forgiveness into their modern lives. What they discovered then was often a sense of release. It was as though they had been wanting and needing this atonement without knowing what it was they wanted and needed. Except in the most perfunctory usage, the concepts underlying it are so archaic that we seldom even fantasize about them. But the need for this kind of release can't be banished just because apology and forgiveness are not "cool."

The sense of release is clearest in the person receiving the apology. It is as though some deep mute force has been holding onto the grievance in spite of all conscious efforts to put it aside, and that what that silent stubborn force has been waiting for is the atonement ritual. When the apology is accepted, the release from long-standing pain is sometimes so powerful that it can be seen physically as some tension in the body lets go in relief.

The release in the person apologizing is more subtle, but nonetheless visible and crucial. Just as the wronged person feels deeply dissatisfied before the apology, so does the person who caused the harm. When I have wronged you, however much I might push down the awareness, somewhere in my body, somewhere in the depths of my mind, I know that something between us is unfinished and disturbing.

Dimly or clearly, both of us perceive some discomfort in ourselves. The relationship needs something, and our emotional well-being needs something, but our repertoire doesn't seem to include that something, whatever it may be. That "something" is of course atonement in both senses of the word. The relationship needs to be "at-oned," and our emotions need to be released from the trauma by amends being made. Why, then, do we block atonement from our list of possibilities? Why is it such a forbidden topic in this culture?

What Holds Us Back?

Readers who have gotten this far will have no trouble answering that question. Our culture is deeply mired in the win-lose view of the world. We have seen how that view makes it difficult for us to have a conversation about ideas without argument. We have seen how hard that view makes it to talk about our relationship without tumbling into the question of who is right and who is wrong. Atonement runs into the same mire.

When I am confronted, I automatically catapult myself into perceiving the situation as a win or a loss. I have been here often; I have seen so many football games and macho movies that this way of perceiving is more familiar than any other. Thus it is extremely difficult for me to see the situation in any other light. I must stand up to the antagonist. I must win if possible, but at all costs I must not lose. A grumbling standoff is not so bad, but to retreat from the fray marks me as weak and unworthy. Therefore, I dare not even consider the rights and wrongs of the case. Were I to do that, the very hesitation while I pondered would be seen as cowardice, and, worse, if I were to discover that I am in the wrong, admitting this would be unthinkable. For then I would be seen as backing down and slinking away while the audience, real or imagined, heaped shame on me.

Given all this, saying "I am in the wrong, I apologize, please forgive me" is a clear one-downer. It is in fact one of the classic one-downers. Popular literature (and modern politics) are full of confrontations in which one antagonist demands an apology from another. Refusal means brave defiance, whereas acceding and offering the apology is abject defeat. So it's not hard to see why saying "Please forgive me" is apt to be unnerving the first times we try it.

The one-down position of the person apologizing is obvious enough. But why should our skin tend to crawl a little when we find ourselves in the opposite position: that of saying "I forgive you"? Why should that apparently strong position raise the specter of one-down?

One of the most one-down things of all is to get caught playing clumsy, obvious one-up. Saying "I forgive you" raises the fear that I'll sound like I'm assuming the role of God, or at least emperor. Thus "I forgive you" is a vulnerable statement for anyone concerned about his or her cool (i.e., his or her one-up score) since any alert antagonist would make short work of such grandiose behavior. Saying "I apologize and ask you to forgive me" requires trust and courage. It appears that "I forgive you" does also. And so, from this point of view, the inability to offer atonement or to receive it is one more burden with which we are saddled by a win-lose world.

During the sixties, the phrase "cop-out" became popular. It was a serious putdown, conveying a cowardly refusal to stand up for oneself. The phrase is still with us. Originally cop-out had a very specific meaning: *cop* came from the phrase *cop a plea*, meaning to admit a fault and negotiate for appropriate consequences. The fact that cop-out has now come to mean something weak or evasive says a good deal about our attitudes toward admitting we've blown one.

Let's look at one final example.

Jonathan and Annie are coworkers and also quite friendly. Though both are single and some attraction has been apparent between them, they have always kept a careful distance. One day Jonathan greets Annie with "That's a very sexy dress." Annie replies jokingly, "Really, sir!" and the conversation ends. Later she approaches him.

Annie: I didn't like that remark about my dress.

Jonathan: Oh yeah? How come?

Annie: I don't think it's appropriate for one thing because I work here and I shouldn't have to put up with that. And also our relationship is confusing enough to me without your making remarks like that.

Jonathan: *(after a pause)* I can see that. I see both of those reasons why it was upsetting.

Annie: It did upset me. And it made me mad.

This is the key moment in the conversation. Jonathan is embarrassed and would like to get out of the interaction as quickly as possible. He has conflicting attitudes toward what happened. At first it doesn't seem to him to have been such a big deal, but it's clear that it was a big deal to Annie. Further, he begins to wonder if his remark was indeed insensitive. He can escape the difficult situation by saying a perfunctory "I'm sorry" and getting out of there. He is indeed tempted to do that. But he cares about her, and he wants to preserve their friendly relations. And he is aware of feeling progressively more uncomfortable about what he said to her.

Jonathan: Annie, I am really sorry. I feel bad about saying that to you. It was a dumb thing to say, and I won't ever talk to you like that again. I sincerely apologize and would like you to forgive me.

Annie: Thanks. I appreciate that. Of course I forgive you. I'm all over it.

Reading this, one can see the relief Jonathan's apology has given Annie, and one can imagine the tension that would have remained had he not managed to apologize. (Readers of our earlier chapters on relationship conversations will note that it looks like it's time for Jonathan and Annie to get some clarity on what their intentions are with each other.)

In our contemporary value system, apology and forgiveness are not cool. But to protect and enhance a loving relationship, to maintain friendly relations, and just to behave honorably, these acts are indispensable. It is tempting to wonder what our world would be like if its endless cycles of humiliation and revenge were to give way to a generous humility built around the concept of atonement.

7

Will You Play Hamlet as Mad or Shamming?

Decision Conversations

Throughout this book we have observed how luxurious it is to take part in a conversation in which no decision need be made. People often get into trouble in a relationship conversation or an idea conversation by forgetting that essential truth. There simply is no need for you and me to decide whether Hamlet is mad or whether baseball is a better game than football. Nor need we decide whether you are more right to feel annoyed by something I've said or I am more right to feel hurt that you've misunderstood me. No decision need be made. There is absolutely nothing to argue about. Once grasped, that is a great liberation.

"Perhaps," you may be thinking, "but in fact there are times when a decision must be made. What then?" And you would be quite right. There are indeed times when a decision must be made, when there are mutually exclusive alternatives. You and I can build the case that Hamlet is mad and then turn around and build the opposite case and let it go at that. But if one of us gets to play Hamlet in a community theater production, we are going to have to decide just how crazy to play him. If you are angry that I don't take out the garbage and I feel burdened by your demands, we are both right; we are each the expert on our feelings. But we still need to answer the question: to whom should the garbage detail be assigned? Now a decision does have to be made.

Conversations take place in different contexts too. You and I may have the luxury of making no choice, while others involved with the same issue may feel enormous pressure to decide. There are strong cases to be made for protecting certain animal species and for preserving certain jobs. A good noncombative conversation about those ideas can be had. But at a certain point the government is going to have to make some decisions, and those decisions are not going to be easy ones. So now what?

Let's classify decision conversations into those in which there are no opposing interests and those in which there are. Suppose you are indeed going to play Hamlet, and I am going to direct the production. Neither of us has any particular investment in just how crazy we want the character played; we just want to do the most interesting production we can. In this case we are essentially engaged in an idea conversation. We try on ideas, we build each other's barns, we play with the possibilities until a conception begins to emerge. Decision conversations like this are the easy ones.

Now suppose a different situation: you have long wanted to play Hamlet as very crazy indeed, and I have just as long been wanting to do a production in which a very sane Hamlet is shamming madness. Now it's a different ballgame. The luxury of having a conversation in which no decision need be made has vanished. You and I begin by wanting different things, and, if we are to work together, we are going to have to come to a decision. And we both very much want to make a choice in a way that protects our friendly relationship. After all, we've got a show to do together. After all, we're friends and want each other to feel respected and satisfied. How can we adapt our principles of cooperation and harmony to this new situation? It is this more difficult class of decision conversations that this chapter is about.

Familiar Confusions

Let's begin by noting that here, as elsewhere, the conversation is apt to be confused and impeded by familiar extraneous forces. The desires to be one-up, to be right, to prove one was right in the past, and, of course, to win can all too easily come to seem more important than finding the best decision.

A small software company had been started in a loft by a couple of laid-back computer whizzes and has become reasonably successful. But now it has outgrown its casual beginnings and hires a new manager to help the company operate in ways more appropriate to its larger size.

Like many similar companies, this one had begun and continued to operate on the basis of flexible work schedules. The employees came in when they wanted and left when they wanted. It was understood they would put in at least forty hours a week. Being young and enthusiastic computer people, they often worked through the night and sometimes put in a good deal more than forty hours. But as the company grew, the staff's dedication and responsibility became less dependable, and it started to be clear that some people were slacking off.

This was the situation when the new manager arrived. He hadn't been on the scene more than a few weeks when he called the employees together and announced the end of the flexible schedule policy. From now on work hours were to be from eight to five with an hour for lunch, and time cards were to be punched.

As you might imagine, the employees, many of whom had been with the company almost from the beginning, had some feelings about this announcement. A series of angry meetings followed. You can guess what were some of the motivating feelings on both sides.

Here's how some of the employees saw it:

"Who the hell is he to come in here and tell us how to run an established business?"

"We've been getting along fine without him."

"He's treating us like untrustworthy children. We won't stand being humiliated this way."

"He's going to wreck the morale of this place."

And so on. The manager had his own point of view:

"I am the manager, and what I say goes. I will not be humiliated by being contradicted."

"I have to establish my authority right at the beginning or I will have no power here at all."

"The CEO trusted them, and they let him down. They have been slacking off. They are untrustworthy children, and they need discipline."

This may be an extreme case, but to some extent in most decision conversations the desires to be right, to be one-up, or to win play a major role. Imagine what a different conversation would ensue if both the manager and the employees set out as *collaborators* to figure out what sort of ingenious solution could be invented that would take into account the interests of the employees and those of the company.

Or, imagine, if you will, that a small committee representing the major philosophical points of view of the Republicans and those of the Democrats is sent away to a comfortable retreat facility for a month with instructions to return with a *theoretical* long-term solution to the national budget deficit. The conference is just an exercise. The participants' constituents and contributors will never know who said what. No individual's name will be attached to any aspect of the plan. The group is accompanied by a facilitator who is there to help them keep to agreed-upon ground rules. The first of these rules is that there will be no arguing. (After all, there is nothing to argue about. They are a team of colleagues trying to solve a problem. And when there is a perceived disagreement within the group with something someone has said, he or she is not attacked or challenged. Instead, the task of resolving the disagreement becomes the task of the entire group.) The second ground rule is that the solution must maximize the satisfaction of all interested parties. The third is that the committee will strive for fairness.

Imagine what those conversations would be like. Clearly, they would be radically different from anything we now hear in the Congress, from the administration, or between the two branches. Of course, many irreducible variables would not go away: no ground rule can eliminate the competing needs, serious uncertainties, and drastically limited resources that any serious debate about the deficit must take into account. But the conversations about these problems would be very different. There would be no name calling and no aspersion casting. And there would be no self-assured statements that I am right and you are wrong, that I know the answer and you don't. Freed from these burdens, freed from the specter of the voter and the contributor, imagination and creativity would flourish as they never can under the more familiar conditions.

The group's proposed solution would not be perfect for anybody, but it would almost certainly be a quantum leap ahead of anything so far seriously proposed and several quanta ahead of anything that's likely to actually get done.

And Irreducible Conflicts

Some decisions do present what certainly look like irreducible conflicts. Abortion is a good example. Many anti-abortion people sincerely and passionately believe that life starts with conception and that abortion is therefore murder. Many pro-choice people sincerely and passionately believe that the state has no business telling people what they can do with their own bodies. If the conversation were ever to become civil, much could be done to work toward the interests of both sides: ways of reducing the number of unwanted pregnancies, ways of gently and noncoercively making alternatives available to pregnant women, and so on. But, when all the compromises that can be made have been made, a government nonetheless has to decide whether or not to outlaw abortion.

In issues of this kind, we may well reach a point at which the crucial interests of the two sides cannot be simultaneously served.

Most decisions, however, are not like this. Most decisions seem to be like this because we adopt *positions* and then battle to defend them. As we will see, positions are very different from *interests*.

If you want to vacation at Truro on Cape Cod and I want to go to Marblehead, it is tempting to fight it out, however gently. Does this temptation feel familiar? I am in danger of losing, and so I had better try hard to win. We were all raised to believe there is not likely to be a way to satisfy everybody's interests and leave all parties content. But a moment's reflection reveals that there often is. Suppose you inquire into my reasons for wanting to go to Marblehead and discover that my mother would be close enough to do some baby-sitting for us. It seems I am not enthused about a vacation with no break from the kids. You reflect for a moment and then say, "Ruth and Erik live in Truro. I'll bet they could set us up with a good baby-sitter." I hadn't thought of that; it seems like a good idea. You have sought out my *interest* and by so doing enabled me cheerfully to abandon my *position*.

If we redefine the task for a decision conversation as that of making the decision as satisfying as possible for all the parties, that new definition changes the situation from an adversarial one to one in which, as in an idea conversation, we all pool our intelligence and creativity toward a common goal. This definition means the difference between you saying to me "You have no imagination. You always want to go to Marblehead" and saying "Let's find out what it is we both want and see whether we can't arrive at a solution."

In exploring idea and relationship conversations, we arrived at some basic principles: the culture teaches us to regard conversations as win-lose situations. You are right or I am right. Your feelings are justified or mine are. We saw that it was neither necessary or helpful to treat conversations that way. We saw that it was possible to enrich our conversational life by reexamining the cultural bias toward win-lose, one-up, and one-down. It is going to be trickier for us to extend those principles to decision conversations, because, as we have seen, sometimes push does indeed come to shove. Nonetheless it can be done. At the very least it can be done a good deal more than we customarily do it.

In exploring idea conversations, we learned to change the model of *debate* to one of *collaborators* trying to build the richest idea possible. In relationship conversations, we learned to change the model from a one-up duel to that of empathic partners trying to increase their understanding of each other. It follows that in decision conversations we will change the model from *antagonists* trying to defeat each other to one of *teammates* trying hard to invent the solution that best serves all the relevant interests.

Getting to Yes

Some years ago, Roger Fisher and William Ury of the Harvard Negotiation Project worked out techniques for taking the battle out of decision conversations. They published these in a remarkable book called *Getting to Yes*. *Getting to Yes* did for decision conversations what we have been attempting in the earlier chapters to do for idea and relationship conversations: change combatants into cooperative problem solvers.

As we examine their method, you are likely to find yourself thinking that it all sounds wonderful—but only as long as the other side is willing to play by these same rules. But what if they aren't? This problem is no different from the same one that arose in studying idea and relationship conversations. The method that Fisher and Ury developed is designed to help you keep the conversation on track even when the other person starts out from an antagonistic stance. And should he or she turn out to be totally inflexible, Fisher and Ury have a way of dealing with that too. Let's examine their method.

Of the techniques around which they build their system, three of them are of particular relevance to us.

1. Separate the people from the problem.

2. Focus on interests, not positions.

3. Invent options for mutual gain.

1. Separate the People from the Problem.

It is not the people against whom you are struggling; it is the problem. And that is true for both sides.

Alma and Joseph are having difficulties in their marriage. Joseph thinks they should go to a marriage counselor, but Alma doesn't want to go. She thinks that the problem is Joe's and that he should seek individual counseling.

As this couple faces this decision, it seems to them that they are antagonists: each of them wants different things, and, for the moment, they seem at odds. They could, however, frame it a different way: in actuality they are partners with a common problem. The common problem is of course that they want different things and are somehow going to have to come to terms with that conflict.

The first move toward separating the people from the problem is to invoke an old friend of ours: empathy. I have to make a real effort to put myself in the other person's shoes, to try hard to grasp her position. This is a strong signal to her that I am not out to thwart her, but rather to help find a solution that takes her needs into account.

> *Joseph:* Honey, I really do understand that you don't want to be involved in any counseling we do. As far as you're concerned, the problem is that I'm not in touch with my emotions, and if I got better about that, you think that would solve the problem. If we went into marriage counseling together, you're afraid that it would be like an admission that our problems are in part your fault. Do I have that right?
>
> *Alma:* That's right. I do all the work toward intimacy in this relationship. Couples' counseling would just be more of the same.
>
> *Joseph:* I know you feel that way. But it would feel really awful for me to go by myself. It makes me the whole problem, and I don't think any one person is ever the whole problem in a marriage.
>
> *Alma:* I guess that's true. Well, I wonder if there's some way we could work this out.

The problem has been separated from the people. These are no longer antagonists but partners with a common problem.

We will return to this couple.

This is a good place to note that the methods advocated by Fisher and Ury explicitly do *not* involve caving in to keep the peace. We are urged to be empathic and understanding, to recognize that the other person has legitimate needs, and to do our best to find a solution that takes those needs into account. *But* we are also urged to hold fast to our principles and, however gently, to insist that our needs are met too. Their mantra for this concept is "Soft on the people, firm on the problem."

2. Focus on Interests, Not Positions.

This is one of the most powerful of Fisher and Ury's insights. A *position* is something on which I've decided. The *interest* is the reason for that decision. For every interest, there are several positions that would satisfy it. Positions may be incompatible. Interests may well not be. When a conversation begins with the statement of incompatible positions, it usually looks as though we are at an impasse. The revelation of the underlying interests may well change that perception radically.

A student-faculty group is engaged in planning an experimental college when the question of independent studies is raised.

A student makes an impassioned speech strongly urging that a student should be allowed to do whatever interests him or her and claim whatever credit seems appropriate to the learning.

A faculty member speaks equally passionately, arguing that independent study should be approved by a faculty member and that the faculty is the appropriate judge of how much credit any academic activity is worth.

The student tells the professor that he is being authoritarian and old-fashioned. The professor calls the student lazy and anti-intellectual. Others join in. The volume is high and the tempo fast. Not only does a group solution appear unlikely (which simply means that the college administration will go ahead and make an arbitrary decision), but relations among the participants appear in danger of being significantly damaged.

Now suppose a sophisticated facilitator asks the members of this group to set aside their positions for a moment and share their interests.

The student's interests: the student very much wants this to be a college where the learners will have some say in the shape of their own learning, where they are respected as important influences. He also wants to be respected in this meeting and not be put down before his comrades. He fears that the faculty is taking them back to the old way in which he would once more be just an object and that this meeting will be symbolic of that if he is proven to be powerless here.

The professor's interests: the professor is afraid that they are on the verge of creating a Mickey Mouse college with students being given credit for listening to rock and roll. He is also afraid of failing to meet what he sees as his legitimate academic responsibilities and of cheapening the degree he really cares about. On the other hand, he shares the student's hopes that this can be a different kind of college in which learners play a major role in planning their own learning. And he too has some anxiety about being ridiculed by his colleagues and humiliated in front of this group.

You can see what a different situation we now have. Before, the positions seemed to be leading to an ever-hardening impasse; now there is a problem to be solved and a lot of very smart people in the room to solve it. All that needs to be done to reach a solution is to invent an option that will take care of student interests and faculty interests. Once freed from the blind struggle, all of the present intelligences can concentrate on this interesting problem.

You will probably be able to think of a number of options in this example. One college solved this problem by inventing the concept of a "study contract" worked out by a student and his or her advisor in which the terms were negotiated until both parties felt satisfied with them.

Thinking up ways to meet diverse interests is sometimes difficult, sometimes very difficult. But dealing with clashing positions is often impossible. Here is the kind of approach that Fisher and Ury suggest we take to this kind of situation:

1. A position is something on which you have decided. (*Students should be the sole determiners of content and credit.*)

2. Your interest is the reason you made that decision. *(I want some influence over my learning process.)*

3. For every interest there are several positions that could satisfy it. Thus the task is to search for the position that meets the interests of both parties.

Behind opposed positions lie shared and compatible interests, as well as opposing ones. This is a very liberating concept.

How, then, shall we anticipate the interests of the other side? The professors might ask themselves:

1. "Why?" and "Why not?" *(Why do the students want to be the sole determiners? Why can't the faculty make those decisions?)*

2. Do they understand what we want? *(Probably not. They must think we want much more control than we actually do.)*

3. How are they likely to see the consequences of meeting our interests? *(They probably think: if we're not careful, we will wind up with no influence.)*

4. What are the interests of the students' constituents? *(The students want their representatives to get them as much power as possible.)*

If one enters a decision conversation having pondered these questions, one is in a good position to facilitate a mutually satisfactory solution.

Once in the conversation we are advised:

1. Explain your interests clearly and inquire about theirs. Never imply that their interests are not legitimate.

2. Acknowledge their interests as part of the problem to be solved. It helps a great deal if they think you have understood their interests.

3. Delay discussing proposals until both sides have fully understood the interests that need to be met.

Recall Fisher and Ury's mantra: "Soft on the people, firm on the problem." "Firm on the problem" means that though we don't commit to a position, we do commit ourselves to our interests. This stimulates creativity in thinking up mutually advantageous solutions. "Soft on the people" means that, as in all the kinds of conversation we have considered in this book, the people are not the antagonists. The people on the other side of a decision conversation are really on your side, in that you are partners trying to solve a problem together—the problem of creating a solution sufficiently ingenious to meet, as far as possible, all the relevant interests. It is the same principle of converting an idea conversation from an argument to a collaborative search for understanding, or converting a relationship conversation from a conflict into a cooperative search for mutual empathy.

So we listen with courteous respect, show empathy, express appreciation for the time and effort they are investing in the conversation, and emphasize our concern for meeting their basic needs. We make it clear we are attacking the problem, not them. The more vigorous we are in presenting our interests, the more supportive we are of the other side.

So we are firm on our interests and supportive of the people. We state our interests clearly and sincerely invite them to share theirs.

Let's return to Joseph and Alma.

Joseph: I don't want to feel like I am the whole problem. That makes me feel hopeless. And to tell the truth, I feel okay about my life. I feel good about this relationship. I know you don't, but I do. And I'm totally willing to work on it, because I want you to be happy.

Alma: I'm afraid that if we go into counseling together it will be like all our other conversations where I do all the talking about feelings and relationships. If I weren't there that wouldn't happen. Then you could get an experience of exploring those parts of yourself.

Now Joseph and Alma are no longer presenting opposed positions. They are beginning to explore the interests that gave rise to the positions. The problem is not solved, but the impasse has been considerably softened.

3. Invent Options for Mutual Gain.

When we studied idea conversations, we saw that much of the fun lay in challenging ourselves to create ideas that integrated or synthesized apparently opposing ideas. When we studied relationship conversations, we saw that, since each person is the expert on his or her own emotions, the challenge lay in understanding that both sets of feelings were true and legitimate. The analog to those concepts in decision conversations may be the most interesting and challenging point of all. Here we are asked to convert a competitive struggle into a collaborative creation, one that will change an apparent impasse into an ingenious solution meeting the most important needs of both sides.

The medieval alchemists strived to turn lead into gold. This phase of decision conversations is the alchemy of interpersonal life.

Sometimes we will succeed wonderfully and rejoice in our creativity; sometimes we will succeed well enough and experience relief; sometimes we will fail. The attempt is always well worth our effort.

A professional football player and the team owner have to make decisions about the player's salary. The process used to go like this: the player's agent would extol the virtues of the player and ask for a large salary. The owner would point out the player's limitations and suggest a much smaller one. The whole basis of the discussion seemed to be that there was a straight line between the two offers and that the final solution, if indeed there was to be one, would have to lie somewhere between the two offers on that straight line.

> *Agent:* He's going to average 5 yards a carry for you. He's a bargain at $700,000.

Owner: It's very unlikely that he will average 5 yards. He averaged 3.8 last year. He's lucky to get $450,000.

And so it would go until they either hammered out a figure in between or reached an impasse.

Then one spring, facing an intractable deadlock, some genius said, "Look. We'll give him a salary of $500,000. If he does indeed average 5 yards a carry, we'll give him a $150,000 bonus."

And ever since, that whole new way of finding options has been standard in sports negotiations.

When Israel and Egypt met at Camp David in 1978 to decide on the fate of the Sinai Peninsula, which Israel had occupied since capturing it in 1967, their positions were incompatible. Israel insisted on keeping some of the Sinai. Egypt wanted it all back. All attempts to work out how much of the Peninsula would be returned to Egypt failed. Egypt wanted it all and would settle for nothing less. Giving up all of it was totally unacceptable to Israel. Impasse.

However, when the interests behind the positions were surfaced, it turned out that Israel's interest was *security*. The Israelis did not want the Egyptian army on their border. Egypt's interest was *sovereignty*. Sinai had been a part of Egypt since the pharaohs, and Egypt was not about to relinquish it. Now that the interests are clear, you can see that it was not that hard to invent options for mutual gain. Give Egypt *sovereign* control over a *demilitarized* Sinai. The Egyptian flags would fly, and there would be no tanks on Israel's border. Alchemy! The lead of impasse had been turned into the gold of a workable decision.

Four obstacles can prevent us from inventing options:

1. Premature criticism or judgment (*I'll look stupid if I suggest that*).

2. The assumption that there is only one solution to the problem and that it won't be solved unless that single solution is found.

3. The assumption that the pie to be divided is fixed in size and that the more you get, the less I get.

4. The belief that "solving their problem is their problem." To arrive at a solution they can accept, we need to help them get their interests taken care of. Often our emotional involvement makes that difficult.

Thus in order to invent creative options, we will need to deal with those four obstacles.

1. We will consciously separate inventing options from judging them. This means brainstorming. A brainstorming session is one in which it is agreed that ideas will be thrown on the table and recorded with no judgment or criticism. Doing so frees the creative process. All ideas are welcome, no matter how far out. When all the ideas have been noted, we can go on to examine the ideas we've collected to see which of them may contain promise.

2. We will broaden our range of options rather than search for a single answer. We tend to think that our *common* interests facilitate agreement and our *differing* interests inhibit it. While it is certainly true that the common interests are to our advantage (*Egypt and Israel both wanted peace*), once we have broadened our range of options, the differences are often what make agreement possible (*Israel wanted security and Egypt wanted sovereignty*). We will search for a solution that capitalizes on those differences.

3. We will search for mutual gains. It is important to free ourselves from the idea that the size of the pie is fixed and that I lose everything you win. The salary dispute involving the football player is a good example. As long as the decision is about how much salary, the size of the pie is fixed—the bigger the slice the player gets, the smaller the size of the pie left for the franchise. But once the salary-plus-incentive bonus is invented, everybody can get something they want.

4. We will invent ways to make their decisions easy. Since all of us want to arrive at a decision, their problems are our problems. So we will put ourselves in their shoes. Do they have a superior they have to convince? Do they have a constituency to please? We will try to imagine how they might be criticized for the decision we reach and work with them to find ways to deal with such criticism. Remember, they are our teammates, not our antagonists. Their problems are our problems. So we search for options to make their job easier.

Joseph and Alma began with only two options: they go into counseling together, or Joseph goes alone. Neither option was acceptable to both. Once positions had been set aside and interests surfaced, it became clear that other options could be considered.

> *Alma:* Suppose we were to do both: suppose we went into counseling together, and you got yourself an individual therapist as well.

> *Joseph:* I don't know if we could afford that. But I want you to know how much I appreciate your willingness to do that.

> *Alma:* Well, if we couldn't afford it, maybe we could do alternate sessions: one week we'd go together, and one week you'd go alone.

> *Joseph:* That still feels like I'm the problem. If I were willing to have individual sessions, would you be willing to have them too?

> *Alma:* You mean one week together, the next week you, and the next week me? Sure, I guess that would be all right. I appreciate your being willing to have individual sessions. If you're willing to have them, it does seem fair that I have them too.

> *Joseph:* I appreciate that.

From the outset the reader will have gathered that this is a book about seeking and achieving harmony. Whether in idea conversations, relationship conversations, or decision conversations, throughout the book we have taken the position that there is nothing to argue about, that harmony is achievable. I hope it has become clear that in idea conversations and relationship conversations a skillful conversationalist can achieve this goal almost irrespective of what the other person does. It takes two to make a struggle.

What Fisher and Ury have shown us is that this is often true in decision conversations as well. However, it is also the case that in decision conversations it is not always true. There are times when even a great deal of skill and good will are not enough to resolve competing interests. What do we do then?

What Are Our Options?

First, we need to know in advance what our options are if we cannot reach a decision that meets our basic interests.

If a decision conversation is an important one, and if it involves the resolution of conflicting interests, it is important to go into the conversation knowing what we will do in case we cannot reach an agreement. Fisher and Ury call this our *Best Alternative to a Negotiated Agreement,* or our BATNA. The better our BATNA, the more we are protected against accepting a decision that does not meet our interests. It is very good for our mental health to begin such a conversation knowing that, if all else fails, we have an acceptable alternative.

Our football player knew he had an offer from another team that he could live with if he had to. That knowledge gave his agent maneuvering room and the awareness that he need not settle for too low a compensation.

The faculty who were engaged in planning the experimental college had a very strong BATNA: if all else failed, they believed they could get a decision from the administration that would be acceptable to them. To counter that alternative, the students in the planning group will want to have the strongest possible BATNA of their own to keep from being forced into an unacceptable decision. The student's BATNA might be to boycott the planning process, call a student protest, appeal to the administration over the faculty's heads, and so on.

Burdensome as the long-term standoff was, Egypt and Israel both knew that they could continue to live with it if they had to, so neither was going to accept a hurtful decision.

The BATNA is the ultimate criterion that determines whether or not we can go along with a given decision. Thus in a situation which we anticipate might produce irresolvable conflict, or in a decision conversation with someone who seems to have the big battalions on his or her side, it is particularly important to determine the very best BATNA we can invent.

And What If They Simply Won't Play?

If the other side plays hardball, insists on a position, or attacks us personally, we're on familiar ground. We're at that point in an idea conversation where the other person insists on arguing. In that familiar situation, we simply built his barn and tried to invite him into a different kind of discussion. We can do the same thing here, always remembering the proviso that when the chips are down we have some significant interests that need to be met.

If they push at us it's tempting to push back. But we're not going to do that, any more than a skillful judo master pushes back. We won't join them in positional bargaining. That would simply lock them in to their position and lock us in to ours. How can we adapt the barn-building principles without abandoning our interests?

1. We neither accept nor reject their offered position. We treat it with interest as one possible option. We look for the interests behind it and try hard to improve it.

2. We invite criticism and advice for our ideas and try to rework our ideas accordingly. We remember that every

interest has many positions that can meet it. We remind them of our interests and ask their advice about how we might accomplish those in a way that works better for them.

3. We reframe attacks on us as attacks on the problem.

Through all this we ask as many questions as possible. Questions allow them to help us understand their interests. Questions offer no target to attack the way statements do.

We ask them if our facts are correct and show that we're open to persuasion. And we present our proposals not as *ours,* but as a fair option that deserves joint consideration. That reduces any ego struggle that's going on.

When confronted with a decision conversation, much of the time, maybe most of the time, we will be able to interest the other person in the three principles:

Separate the people from the problem.

Focus on interests, not positions.

Invent options for mutual gain.

We will be able to do this because it is so clearly to our mutual advantage to do so. To the extent we succeed in doing so, we maximize the possibility of a wise and fair decision.

An 82-year-old woman has had a serious stroke and is not conscious. She has just been taken to the hospital. She has two children, Nicholas and Laurie. Laurie happens to be a ward nurse at another hospital. They sit in the visitor's lounge of the ward. The doctor finds them there.

Doctor: I'm afraid your mother is not in very good shape. She has sustained major brain damage. Her heart and her other vital organs seem to be in fairly good shape, considering her age. I think she is in no immediate danger of dying if we put a feeding tube in her. But I very much doubt she will regain consciousness, or, at least if she does momentarily, I am practically certain she will not be able to communicate or even to recognize you. Has your mother left any directive about how vigorously she wants to be treated in a condition like this?

Nicholas: No, she hasn't

Doctor: Well, in that case it's up to you two. If you decide to put a feeding tube in her, I don't know how long she will live, perhaps for many months. If we don't do that, she will die very soon.

Laurie: What's your advice, Doctor Martin?

Doctor: I can't give you advice. But I will tell you that if she were my mother I would not put a tube in her . . . We should make the decision in a couple of days.

Laurie: Thanks, Doctor Martin. We'll let you know tomorrow.

The doctor leaves.

Laurie: *(takes Nicholas's hand)* Nicholas, I know how hard this is going to be for you . . . I think we should not put the tube in.

Nicholas: *(in tears)* I don't know what you mean. You mean just kill her?

Laurie: *(now also in tears)* Nick, she's already dead. It's simply cruel to force her to hang on like this.

Nicholas: There's a Papal encyclical on this. We are required by God's law to do everything we can to keep her alive.

Laurie: Nick, could we talk about what "alive" means? I'd like to see if we can work this out so we can agree.

Nicholas: I'm not going to agree to kill my mother. I'm not ever going to agree. I want her kept alive as long as possible. Look . . . Did it every occur to you that the doctor could be wrong and that she could wake up?

I mean *really* wake up? Did that ever occur to you? Much stranger things than that have happened.

They are silent for some moments.

Laurie: Do you think you could tell me exactly what it means to you to keep Mom's body alive? I really want us to do what's best for her and both of us. I understand you're hoping for a miracle recovery and also that you have a religious problem about not putting in a feeding tube. Is that right? Are those your concerns?

Nicholas: Those are certainly two of them.

Laurie: Nick, you're a reasonable man. Suppose we ask Doctor Martin if there's any remote theoretical chance that Mom could wake up, I mean *really* wake up. We could ask him not for his opinion, but simply if it's *possible*. Would it be good to have that information?

Nicholas doesn't answer.

Laurie: What do you think, Nick? Wouldn't it be good to at least know that before we make a decision?

Nicholas: Laurie, she's our mother. Don't you love her?

Laurie: I love her, and I love you. It's one of the hardest decisions we are ever going to be called upon to make and I want to make it carefully so that we take the best possible care of Mom and also of you and me . . . I would really be grateful if we could talk to Doctor Martin again and ask him that. Let's make this decision as wisely as we can.

Nicholas: But, whatever he says, killing her is against God's will.

Laurie: You know more religion than I do. I imagine it's a very subtle theological question. I would be really glad for us to go see Father McCarroll together and get his opinion.

Nicholas is silent.

Laurie: Nicholas, it's really important that we get together on this. If we disagree, I don't know what the doctor will do.

Nicholas: I don't think he would dare withhold the tube if I said no—whatever you said.

Laurie: If we disagreed, I could go to the hospital ethics committee and ask them to let Mom die. I have no idea what they'd do, but in any case I really don't want to do that. You are my brother, and I am determined we are going to work this out together . . . Can I ask you something?

Nicholas: Yes.

Laurie: If we put a tube in Mom, she's going to go to a nursing home and be there indefinitely—just lying there unconscious till she dies. Had you thought how we're going to pay for that?

Nicholas: Medicaid will pay for it.

Laurie: Medicaid will only pay for it when she has no assets. And that means they'll take the house . . . I know how much you love her and what a wonderful son you've been to her—much better than the daughter I've been to her . . . And I know you want to continue to be good to her. But how is it going to feel to you to see her day after day the way she is now? Is that really going to feel like we're keeping her alive? I need you to know that I would feel absolutely dreadful thinking of her ending her beautiful life like that. Can you show me a different way to think about that? Nick, I want to do what's best for us all. And I know you would do anything to keep her alive. We have to think hard about whether she is really alive now or whether we're doing some cruel thing to her body.

Nicholas is silent.

Laurie: How about we do this: let's get some data. Let's talk to Doctor Martin and to Father McCarroll. I agree to be influenced by them. If Doctor Martin thinks there is any possibility of her recovering or if Father McCarroll advises us to put in the feeding tube, I will agree to go along. And if they both support our withholding the tube, I ask you to agree.

Nicholas: You know the doctor will agree. He's already said so.

Laurie: We're not going to ask his opinion. We're going to ask him if it's possible that she will recover.

Nicholas: *(after a long pause)* Okay, Laurie. I'll agree to that.

Barn raising can be contagious. When I don't argue with you, but build your idea, it often interests you in trying an alternative to argument. Similarly, talking about one's own feelings can be contagious: when I don't tell you what's wrong with you, but just how I feel, you may be drawn into responding in kind. In the same way, when approaching a difficult decision with someone who is dug in, principled negotiation can prove contagious.

8

Can I Really Do This at Work?

Conversations in the Business Environment

Readers who spend their days in a business environment may well be wondering by now how the points of view in this book might apply there. Those of us who spend eight hours a day in workplace settings are well aware that the conversations that take place on the job or in the office are a lot less satisfying than they might be. If I offer a point of view different from a colleague or a superior, it is apt to be ignored or argued with. If some interpersonal difficulty arises, there is apt to be a tense exchange and perhaps no resolution. And since we spend forty hours or more out of every week at work, those conversations are apt to have a significant impact on the quality of our lives.

Quality of life is the concern of this book. Yet personal growth and organizational change are very different endeavors. I may have learned how to have extraordinarily interesting conversations with friends or at home, but do I dare take these same principles to work? How will I be seen if I barn-build with my colleagues? What will happen if I try to tell my boss how I'm feeling? Could these principles provide a way to improve business conversation so that it's both more productive and more human?

It seems to be acknowledged in the most progressive business circles that something had better improve business conversation. No less an authority than Alan Webber, former editor of the *Harvard Business Review*, says, "Conversation is the means by which people share and often create what they know. Therefore the most important work in the new economy is creating conversations."

So let's see if the principles we have been exploring in this book can be of help in creating a new kind of conversation for people whose business is business.

The most apparent use to which this book can be put by businesspeople is in decision making. Negotiating decisions goes on almost continuously between companies and between departments, and employing the guidelines of principled negotiation would take a good deal of the stress out of it and hopefully lead to more profitable outcomes as well. But what about the other kinds of conversation we have been examining? What about idea conversations and relationship conversations? Can they be of use in evolving the new kind of creative conversation that Alan Webber says is indispensable to the new economy?

When it comes to exploring ideas at work, four problems appear likely to get in the way of a truly fruitful collaboration.

1. Competitive Assertiveness

The present situation in many businesses is less than ideal. The air of competitiveness makes the workplace less pleasant and less nurturing than it could be. And equally important is the cost to productivity and creativity as naked competition diverts a good deal of energy from the goals of the organization.

You may recall the new manager from chapter 7 who barged into the software company and set a new work-hours policy. Let's suppose that he actually had a bit more tact and instead of simply laying down a new policy, he started by calling a meeting of the workforce. Let's remember that, in addition to having a real stake in the decision, all the employees in the meeting are aware that this is one of their first opportunities to impress a new superior.

Ken, the new manager, opens the meeting:

Ken: As I mentioned in my memo, we have a problem. Not everybody is putting in the time they get paid for. So how do we deal with that?

Bob: I don't believe there's a problem. I think we're fixing something that ain't broke.

Ann: I'm not sure that's true, Bob. I know that . . .

Bill: I don't think the issue is whether or not there's a problem. The issue is should we have a new system of accountability.

Bob: Of course the issue is whether or not there's a problem. Why on earth would we even want to consider a new system if there's nothing wrong with this one?

Bill: You're going about this in the wrong order.

That kind of conversation is familiar to all of us.

In Deborah Tannen's study of business conversation, *Talking from 9 to 5,* she notes instance after instance where assertive people tend to drown out less assertive ones. Women who take dominant roles are not as well liked as women who remain more passive, and since women like to be liked they are reluctant to appear dominant. Tannen reports that in the present climate, a man who is not assertive—or even something less than aggressively assertive—is likely to go unrecognized and not be seen as competent, however competent he may actually be. Women who are generous, nurturant, and supportive are liked, but are seen as minor players and are not given much influence. Both men and women are likely to be defeated in negotiations if they value harmony and empathy. The winners are apt to be the aggressive stonewallers.

What this means is that even though the company is paying for the thoughts and the ideas of all its employees, it is not getting the use of them. If business conversations could be aimed at producing the highest possible morale and the most creative solution, this change would have a marked positive effect on the bottom line.

Let's quickly acknowledge that people in business are faced with troublesome conflicts as they consider ways of conversing. They want to be as productive as possible. They want to live in a nurturing environment. And they want to get ahead. At a glance, it seems apparent that these goals are sometimes going to be in conflict. Whether you want to be competitively assertive or supportively nurturing, in either case you have to be aware that your contributions are being observed and will have a marked effect on your career. When linguists like Deborah Tannen study the business environment they discover (to no one's very great surprise, I guess) that the usual customs of business conversation are not calculated to maximize either productivity or a pleasant environment.

I can imagine a very primitive manager responding to this news by growling that he's not running a nursery school, and if people want their ideas heard they'd better just fight to get them heard. This position is primitive not only because of its human implications, but also because of what it does to the success of the company. As we noted above, when a worker's ideas get shut out, the company is paying for a resource not fully available to it. If the conversational culture of the company is typical, it is likely that the company is being deprived of a significant amount of resources, resources it can ill afford to lose. That is why Alan Webber says that it is time for businesses to begin encouraging a new kind of conversation.

2. Rush to Decision

There are pressures in every business conversation to make the decision and get on with it. There are always time pressures and almost always someone pressing the group for a decision. Decisiveness is also a virtue highly valued among businesspeople; thus many workers fear that if they don't look decisive, it will count against them. That is a very expensive attitude, and, as our business world becomes more and more complex and less and less amenable to the old solutions, it will become an even more costly attitude.

It is rare that a group can make the best decision in a hurry. And the issue is not just time; it is opportunity for the members to stimulate each other's creativity. As we saw in the chapter on decision conversations, there are always more options than first appear.

> *Mac:* Look, either we put in time clocks or we don't. I'm sick of being suspected of freeloading. Let's just put in time clocks and be done with it.
>
> *Sally:* I'm sick of the whole thing. I agree. Let's do it.

3. Criticism and Attack

As we saw in an earlier chapter, people do not think well when under attack. Thus a conversation characterized by the criticism of each other's ideas is not likely to be one that produces the best possible solution to the problem. In addition, going into a meeting knowing that the knives will be out is not calculated to make a worker eager to attend the meeting. Nor is being regularly subjected to such meetings calculated to improve one's mental health. So if meetings characterized by criticism and attack do not produce the best solutions, and if they are not much fun for the workers, why are they so common?

At least part of the problem is the old business culture that says, "We're tough, we're no-nonsense. We ask no quarter and we give none. This is the real world, and if you can't stand the heat stay out of the kitchen." I don't think that there's any doubt that the business world would be a good deal more livable were this part of the culture to change. And I think more and more managers are realizing that times have changed and a new ethic is gong to be necessary.

> *Judy:*   Mac, that's a bad idea. Try to think it through a little. That would have a terrible effect on the place.
>
> *Mac:*   I haven't heard you come up with a better one.
>
> *Judy:*   I think we should leave it like it is.
>
> *Mac:*   That's just dumb. They're not going to leave it like it is, and you know it.

4. The Need to Score

Coaches and sophisticated observers of all sports are vividly aware that the game is not won just by the player who scores, but also by the player who makes the score possible. In basketball and hockey the assist may be a perfect pass or a perfectly timed screen. In football it may be the block that springs the runner loose, or the player who gets in the way of the cornerback, enabling a spectacular reception. That kind of sophistication is still lacking in business conversations.

Tannen reports instance after instance in which one person gets all the credit for an idea when the development of that idea clearly depended on the preceding conversation. In fact, she reports, the entire idea may well have been offered by a previous speaker who is less assertive and dominating than the one who actually gets credit for it.

> *John:* Maybe it would be good to keep our options open and not just rush into deciding that our only two choices are time clocks or nothing. Maybe there's some other way to think about it.

> *Ann:* I think that's right. Maybe we could make and enforce some kind of system among ourselves that would take care of the problem.

> *John:* Right. I would love to keep the management out of it.

> *Judy:* Well, one way . . .

> *Bill:* (*with some enthusiasm*) Why don't we work out an honor system? If we could do it, that would take care of the problem without getting into a sweatshop scene.

> *Ken:* Bill, I think that's a really good idea. Let's think how we can implement Bill's idea.

What Can Be Done?

In contrast with relationship conversations (which we'll look at in a moment), it seems likely that for there to be dramatic change in the corporate culture, much of the impetus must come from the top—from the head of a unit or a division, if not from the top of the company. It may be asking too much of an individual employee to build a colleague's barn and to generously let credit go to others, when her advancement in the company is likely to suffer. We will see in a moment that there are some things the individual worker can do to change the culture. But it does seem that much of the change must come with the sanction of management.

Since the main corporate goal is the company's success, it should be of considerable interest to managers that the present corporate culture does less to promote that goal than it might. A major manifestation of that failing is the way conversation is conducted. In the current culture, managers are not always able to recognize which of their people have creative contributions to make; thus they may not select the best person for a given assignment. And perhaps worst of all, the company does not have access to the best ideas of its employees. This is dramatically evident in the case of women employees.

Tannen says:

> The skills girls are more likely to have learned, such as linking one's comments to those of others, waiting to be recognized rather than speaking out, making suggestions rather than demands, supporting others' remarks rather than making all one's comments sound original, are very constructive when everyone at the meeting is observing those rituals. But they may not help a speaker stand out—or even get the floor—at a meeting. And there are good reasons why speaking up and being the center of attention in a group, especially a group that includes men, is a more difficult and complicated matter for women, since so much of their socialization has taught them not to attract attention. All these patterns make meetings more congenial for more men than women. (*Talking from 9 to 5*, p. 301)

Thus some significant portion of the ideas of a company's female employees are shut out. Managers must certainly care about the effect this has on the bottom line. And it is to be hoped they also care about the considerable effect this has on the self-esteem of the women who work for them.

Tannen also observes that in unstructured meetings it is not just the women who get shut out, though the women do indeed tend to get short-changed. Any employee, male or female, who tends to be quiet or who values listening and supporting others more than pushing his ideas forward will not be heard as much as the more forceful members, and consequently the ideas of those quiet members are not likely to be available to the meeting and thus to the company.

Though corporate managers may not always realize it, job satisfaction and self-esteem have a major effect on the company's success. Argumentative meetings are not satisfying, which is one of the reasons so many workers report a strong dislike of meetings. And, since a manager must be concerned with maximizing the creativity of his or her unit, it would seem that creating an environment that encourages the unimpeded flow of new options should have a high priority.

Suppose, then, that a manager were to train his or her unit in the principles of barn raising. An issue comes up; the manager calls a meeting and suggests that before the group decides anything, it treats the issue in question as a topic for an idea conversation. We know from our study of decision conversations that it's useful to expand the options available for us, and this seems like a good way to do it.

Training a unit in barn raising ought to be a good antidote for the four problems we have listed: competitive assertiveness, rush to decision, criticism and attack, and the need to score.

In a barn-raising conversation each speaker is expected to support and enhance the other speakers—thus, in a stroke, eliminating the possibility of being rewarded for competition and attack. And since each speaker attempts to build on the ideas of previous speakers, the assist becomes as important as the score.

So let's suppose that before Ken called the meeting about work hours, he had set up a workshop to train his people in these principles. Let's imagine what that conversation might sound like.

Bob: Do we actually *know* that people have been goofing off?

Ann: (*the president*) Yes, we do. People have acknowledged it to me. I think everybody knows it.

Bill: It's tricky. I think what makes this place good to work at is the informal atmosphere and that we trust each other. It would be a shame to lose that.

Sally: Okay, let's see if there's a way to solve the problem without turning the place into a prison. Could we work out an honor system?

Bob: Isn't that what we have now?

Mac: No, wait, Sally has an idea. We don't really have an honor *system.* We have a kind of laissez faire arrangement.

John: You mean like West Point has an honor system.

Mac: Right, and not just West Point. A lot of regular old colleges have it too. I don't know what it's like now, but my dad told me that years ago at Princeton if a student saw someone cheating in an exam, he would start to stamp his feet and pretty soon everybody would be stamping till the guy cheating stopped or left.

John: It's an interesting idea. The employees would have our own honor committee, and if someone wasn't playing by the rules, the committee would take care of it, and it would never reach management. Then it's all in our hands. No time clock, no policemen.

Judy: It *is* an interesting idea, but isn't there a real problem? We all get along pretty well with each other now and trust each other. Do we want to turn into cops policing each other and lose what sense of unity we have?

John: Okay, we've got a dilemma. We'd like to have the responsibility for work hours stay with us, and we don't want to risk putting a bad vibe into the place. How do we handle that?

Mac: How about a rotating honor committee, so that everybody takes his or her turn? Would that help?

Judy: That might do it. Now the question is what would this committee do if they did find somebody not playing by the rules?

Sally: Talk to them like friends and ask them to straighten up.

Bob: What's the incentive? What's the incentive for the honor committee to bring it up, and what's the incentive for the person to give a damn?

Mac: Oh, I think the incentive all around is that if we don't straighten this out, we're going to get time clocks and this place will not be much fun to work in.

Bob: I think the idea has possibilities. That was a good thought, Sally.

Judy: What do you think, Ann? Would you buy it?

Ann: I'd give it a try.

Sally: Ken?

Ken: Sure. Sounds fine. And I very much appreciate the way you're working together.

Judy: You guys feel all right? You actually listened to the women for a change.

It is probably true that major changes in the climate of meetings will require the cooperation of management. But that does not mean that individuals are powerless to effect change. Though being the first to be generous in idea conversations entails the risk of hiding your potential for promotion under a bushel, judicious modeling of the barn-raising mode might well evoke a corresponding generosity. So a worker might safely take the risk of experimenting with approaches like these:

"That's a good idea; I like that."

"Maybe we can put that together with what Judy said a little while ago."

"Wait a minute, you guys. Don't freeze yourselves
into those positions. Let's see what each of your
interests are and see if we can resolve them. I imagine
we can."

"Let's not try to make a decision yet. Let's see if there
are more possibilities."

While these may seem like very small steps to take, even a
little creativity and collaboration can have a positive impact on
the quality of the ideas generated and, ultimately, the kinds of
decisions that get made. A few successes can help make everyone more open to an approach that generates results. Over the
long term, such experimenting might even inspire the managers
who benefit from it to make significant changes in the culture.
And that would be good for everybody.

Authenticity in Power Relations

It's probably not the best policy to walk up to the boss and, in
the interest of openness, tell him you don't like him. But that
doesn't mean that the rules of relationship conversation can't be
of use at work. We noted that the principles of barn raising
should be applied judiciously unless everybody is playing by
the same rules. The principles of relationship conversation are a
different matter. If you are sensitive to your listener and speak
in a way that he or she can hear, you can talk from your feelings
no matter what the other person is doing. You may or may not
inspire the other person to do the same. In either case you are
apt to emerge from the conversation feeling a good deal more
satisfied.

Let's review a few principles from our study of relationship
conversations.

1. Talking about my feelings helps me stick to talking
   about *me*. Since that is the subject on which I am the
   unqualified expert, there can be no arguing with me.
   Also it sets an example that *may* encourage the other

person to talk about his or her feelings. This is a hopeful condition for resolution since there is now nothing for either of us to argue about.

2. If I talk about my opinions, that is apt to mean that I end up talking about you. There can be a lot of arguing about that.

3. A particularly dicey form of opinion is mind-reading. Telling the other person what he or she was thinking or what their real motive was, is very very likely to stir resentment and make the conversation difficult.

Let's look at a couple of examples.

Ray is Patrick's supervisor on a production unit. He assigns Patrick to present a new product to the sales managers. In the middle of Patrick's presentation, Ray wanders into the room and sits in the back. After some moments he says, "Excuse me, Patrick, I think there's an important aspect you're leaving out." He then takes over and finishes the presentation himself.

Later they meet in Patrick's office.

Ray: I hope you didn't mind my helping you out in there. You were doing okay. I just thought I could clarify it a bit.

Patrick: I think it's hard for you, Ray, to give the spotlight over to any of your people. I don't think that was a great thing you did to me.

Ray: It's not hard for me at all. I like to see the people who report to me have a chance to show what they can do.

Patrick: Then what did you cut in on me like that for?

Ray: I didn't cut in on you. I just saw a way to clarify a couple of your points. Actually, I thought you'd appreciate the help. The point around here isn't personal glory. The point is to get the job done.

> *Patrick:* I knew all that stuff you said. I just hadn't gotten to it yet.
>
> *Ray:* I was just trying to get the job done, Patrick. I don't see what difference it makes who does it.

This conversation has to be very unsatisfying for Patrick. It can't be much better for Ray. And it seems all too likely that something like this will happen again.

Patrick is angry, but he's not saying that he is. Instead he opens by reading Ray's mind, accusing him of a pretty unpleasant motive. That sets the tone for the rest of the conversation, which finally becomes little more than an argument about whether Ray's action was good or bad. Patrick's "I think it's hard for you, Ray, to give the spotlight over to any of your people" is so likely to put Ray on the defensive that from then on a satisfying conversation seems out of reach.

Now, suppose Patrick had approached Ray differently. Suppose he had followed our guidelines for relationship conversations.

> *Ray:* I hope you didn't mind my helping you out in there. You were doing okay. I just thought I could clarify it a bit.
>
> *Patrick:* Ray, I appreciate your coming in to talk to me. As a matter of fact, I did mind it. I felt completely humiliated—just standing there with egg on my face while you took over from me.
>
> *Ray:* You've got it all wrong, Patrick. I didn't want to hurt you or humiliate you. I just wanted to clear up a few points that seemed important.
>
> *Patrick:* I understand that's what you wanted. I'd appreciate it if you hear the effect it had on me. It made me feel embarassed and humiliated, and it made me afraid that every one of those people sees me as incompetent. And it made me very leery of accepting any more assignments like this.

Ray: Well, I certainly didn't want you feeling like that. I'm really sorry, Patrick. I'll be more careful in the future.

Patrick: Thanks; I appreciate that.

In this version Patrick tells Ray how Ray's action made him feel. Ray responds by telling Patrick that he got it wrong, because Ray had no intention of making him feel that way. Patrick gives Ray a fast and effective lesson in the difference between *intent* and *impact*. He accepts Ray's statement of intent and firmly asks Ray to return the courtesy by hearing his statement of impact.

There are at least two possible explanations for Ray's shouldering Patrick out. One is that he is indifferent to his people or even competitive with them. If that is the case, it may take more than Patrick's sharing his feelings to change Ray. On the other hand, Ray might have acted out of mere insensitivity. In that case, Patrick has raised Ray's consciousness, and things may be different in the future. But, in either case, expressing his feelings will hopefully make Patrick feel better, and that is important. He is not left with a frustrating argument.

Let's look at another situation.

Sandra and Noah are coworkers who have become friendly. Sandra is promoted to a spot they both wanted. After some weeks, Noah stops by Sandra's office.

Noah: You hardly speak to me anymore. How come?

Sandra: I don't know. Nothing special. I've just been very busy.

Noah: That's not true, Sandra. You hardly answer me when I say hello. In fact we only talk to each other when we have to.

Sandra: You're exaggerating, Noah.

Noah: I don't think so. Are you feeling guilty about being promoted over me? Is that why you avoid me?

Sandra: I'm not avoiding you. And I don't feel guilty. I think *you're* mad at *me* because of the promotion.

Noah: Is that why you're avoiding me? Cause you think I'm mad at you?

You can see how this will go from here and how it is very likely to leave both people feeling worse than when they started. Neither Sandra nor Noah are talking about their own feelings, and both are mind-reading the other. In a conversation like this, it doesn't matter whether an attempt to read someone's mind is accurate or not. We all like to be given the right to say what's true for us, and not have others attempt to say it for us. In addition, Noah opens with an accusation unaccompanied by any statement of his own feelings. Such an accusation is very likely to put Sandra on the defensive and leave her in a mood too self-protective to allow open communication.

Suppose Noah had approached the conversation differently:

Noah: Sandra, I'm scared that we're losing our friendship since you moved out of the office. It seems to me like you don't talk to me unless we have business together.

Sandra: I don't think that's true. I've just been very busy.

Noah: I know you have, and I can appreciate the pressure you've been under. What troubles me is that you hardly seem to answer me when I say hello.

Sandra: You're exaggerating, Noah.

Noah: Maybe I am. The reason that I'm concerned is that I like you a lot and would hate to lose our friendship. You know, Sandra, I feel quite okay about your being promoted. I don't have any bad feelings about it at all, and I hope that hasn't put something weird between us.

In our first version of this conversation, Noah's attempt to read Sandra's mind ("Are you feeling guilty about being promoted over me?") predictably evoked Sandra's own mind-reading riposte ("I think *you're* mad at *me* because of the promotion"). When Noah approaches Sandra with his feelings openly disclosed, he leaves her a good many more options.

It's possible that she may need to maintain some distance between them. If so, she may decline Noah's generous opening and persist in a mind-reading mode.

> *Sandra:*   I don't know, Noah. I think maybe you *are* mad about the promotion, and that's why you're laying this on me.

However, it is much more likely that generous openness will beget generous openness.

> *Sandra:*   Well, thanks, Noah. To tell you the truth I *have* felt a little funny about it. I'm really glad you decided to talk to me about it.

We have noted that there are limits to how much an individual worker can make changes in idea conversations. No such limits apply in relationship conversations.

Whatever the current climate in a given corporate culture, any individual can do something to change it—to make it less combative and to experience fewer frustrating encounters. Sooner or later *something* is going to have to change it. The new business world will not tolerate primitive conversations forever.

Bibliography

Bradford, Leland, Jack Gibb, and Kenneth Benne, eds. *T-Group Theory and Laboratory Method*. New York: Wiley, 1964.

Buber, Martin. *I and Thou*. New York: Scribners, 1958.

Fisher, Roger, and William Ury. *Getting to Yes*. Boston: Houghton Mifflin, 1981.

Hacker, Andrew. *Two Nations*. New York: Scribners, 1992.

Kohut, Heinz. *How Does Analysis Cure?* Chicago: University of Chicago Press, 1984.

Lakoff, Robin Tolmach. *Talking Power*. New York: Basic Books, 1990.

Potter, Stephen. *The Complete Upmanship*. New York: Holt, Rinehart, and Winston, 1970.

Reps, Paul. *Zen Flesh, Zen Bones*. Rutland, VT: Charles E. Tuttle, 1957.

Rogers, Carl. *On Becoming a Person*. Boston: Houghton Mifflin, 1961.

Tannen, Deborah. *Talking from 9 to 5*. New York: William Morrow, 1994.

Other New Harbinger Self-Help Titles

Preparing for Surgery, $17.95
Coming Out Everyday, $13.95
Ten Things Every Parent Needs to Know, $12.95
The Power of Two, $12.95
It's Not OK Anymore, $13.95
The Daily Relaxer, $12.95
The Body Image Workbook, $17.95
Living with ADD, $17.95
Taking the Anxiety Out of Taking Tests, $12.95
The Taking Charge of Menopause Workbook, $17.95
Living with Angina, $12.95
PMS: Women Tell Women How to Control Premenstrual Syndrome, $13.95
Five Weeks to Healing Stress: The Wellness Option, $17.95
Choosing to Live: How to Defeat Suicide Through Cognitive Therapy, $12.95
Why Children Misbehave and What to Do About It, $14.95
Illuminating the Heart, $13.95
When Anger Hurts Your Kids, $12.95
The Addiction Workbook, $17.95
The Mother's Survival Guide to Recovery, $12.95
The Chronic Pain Control Workbook, Second Edition, $17.95
Fibromyalgia & Chronic Myofascial Pain Syndrome, $19.95
Diagnosis and Treatment of Sociopaths, $44.95
Flying Without Fear, $12.95
Kid Cooperation: How to Stop Yelling, Nagging & Pleading and Get Kids to Cooperate, $12.95
The Stop Smoking Workbook: Your Guide to Healthy Quitting, $17.95
Conquering Carpal Tunnel Syndrome and Other Repetitive Strain Injuries, $17.95
The Tao of Conversation, $12.95
Wellness at Work: Building Resilience for Job Stress, $17.95
What Your Doctor Can't Tell You About Cosmetic Surgery, $13.95
An End to Panic: Breakthrough Techniques for Overcoming Panic Disorder, $17.95
On the Clients Path: A Manual for the Practice of Solution-Focused Therapy, $39.95
Living Without Procrastination: How to Stop Postponing Your Life, $12.95
Goodbye Mother, Hello Woman: Reweaving the Daughter Mother Relationship, $14.95
Letting Go of Anger: The 10 Most Common Anger Styles and What to Do About Them, $12.95
Messages: The Communication Skills Workbook, Second Edition, $13.95
Coping With Chronic Fatigue Syndrome: Nine Things You Can Do, $12.95
The Anxiety & Phobia Workbook, Second Edition, $17.95
Thueson's Guide to Over-the-Counter Drugs, $13.95
Natural Women's Health: A Guide to Healthy Living for Women of Any Age, $13.95
I'd Rather Be Married: Finding Your Future Spouse, $13.95
The Relaxation & Stress Reduction Workbook, Fourth Edition, $17.95
Living Without Depression & Manic Depression: A Workbook for Maintaining Mood Stability, $17.95
Coping With Schizophrenia: A Guide For Families, $13.95
Visualization for Change, Second Edition, $13.95
Postpartum Survival Guide, $13.95
Angry All the Time: An Emergency Guide to Anger Control, $12.95
Couple Skills: Making Your Relationship Work, $13.95
Handbook of Clinical Psychopharmacology for Therapists, $39.95
Weight Loss Through Persistence, $13.95
Post-Traumatic Stress Disorder: A Complete Treatment Guide, $39.95
Stepfamily Realities: How to Overcome Difficulties and Have a Happy Family, $13.95
The Chemotherapy Survival Guide, $11.95
The Deadly Diet, Second Edition: Recovering from Anorexia & Bulimia, $13.95
Last Touch: Preparing for a Parent's Death, $11.95
Self-Esteem, Second Edition, $13.95
I Can't Get Over It, A Handbook for Trauma Survivors, Second Edition, $15.95
Concerned Intervention, When Your Loved One Won't Quit Alcohol or Drugs, $12.95
Dying of Embarrassment: Help for Social Anxiety and Social Phobia, $12.95
The Depression Workbook: Living with Depression and Manic Depression, $17.95
Prisoners of Belief: Exposing & Changing Beliefs that Control Your Life, $12.95
Men & Grief: A Guide for Men Surviving the Death of a Loved One, $13.95
When the Bough Breaks: A Helping Guide for Parents of Sexually Abused Children, $11.95
When Once Is Not Enough: Help for Obsessive Compulsives, $13.95
The Three Minute Meditator, Third Edition, $12.95
Beyond Grief: A Guide for Recovering from the Death of a Loved One, $13.95
Leader's Guide to the Relaxation & Stress Reduction Workbook, Fourth Edition, $19.95
The Divorce Book, $13.95
Hypnosis for Change: A Manual of Proven Techniques, Third Edition, $13.95
When Anger Hurts, $13.95
Lifetime Weight Control, $12.95